Reality is Fabulous

David Bruce

Published by David Bruce, 2023.

While every precaution has been taken in the preparation of this book, the publisher assumes no responsibility for errors or omissions, or for damages resulting from the use of the information contained herein.

REALITY IS FABULOUS

First edition. April 18, 2023.

Copyright © 2023 David Bruce.

ISBN: 979-8223756705

Written by David Bruce.

Table of Contents

Dedication

Dedicated to My Mother

Josephine Bruce, my mother, died at 7:40 p.m. Saturday, 14 June 2003 at Hickory Creek Nursing Center in The Plains.

She could have died a few weeks earlier at Doctors Hospital in Nelsonville, but I made the decision to have her connected to a machine that would breathe for her. In doing this, I went against her wishes that she had very clearly expressed to me previously.

As it happened, this was most likely the right thing to do. She was connected to the breathing machine for less than 12 hours and was then able to breathe on her own until she died Saturday. It was possible that she would have had to stay connected to the breathing machine for the rest of her life.

She forgave me for my decision.

In the additional weeks that remained to her, the most important thing we did together was to write letters to all of her children. The basic message of each letter was the same: I love you and I know that you love me.

When she died, all of her children were with her.

She knew she was dying. When I saw her that morning, I knew that she was very ill and I told her that this might be the day she died. When her doctor arrived, he let her know that she would most likely not survive.

This is exactly the way it should be. If I were dying, I would want to know.

She was not afraid of death. She knew that it was time, and I think that she welcomed it. Like the old song says, as a Christian, she was wearing her traveling shoes. However, like most of us, she was probably afraid that dying might be painful.

Her dying was not painful. Doctors are humane, and pain management is now an advanced art. Morphine took away the pain.

Her dying was fairly quick. Her doctor told me that she would probably die within 12 to 24 hours. From the time he told me that to the time she died took seven and a half hours.

The seven and a half hours were a misery, but to wait 12 to 24 hours for her to die would have been an extended stay in Hell.

When she died, one of her sons was holding her right hand and one of her daughters was holding her left hand. Her other children were gathered around her.

Her death was quiet. The time between each breath grew longer and longer and soon there was no next breath.

One minute she was alive and breathing. The next minute—with no change in her expression—she was dead.

While she was dying, we played her favorite gospel and country music on her stereo. She died as her favorite singer, John Denver, was singing about going home again.

People who live in nursing homes tend to have few opportunities to do good deeds that involve money, but one thing she did was to send flowers to the Hickory Creek Nursing Center kitchen to thank the kitchen workers because she liked the food.

People who live in nursing homes tend to have few possessions. Her most valuable possessions were her music CDs, which—as she requested—her children divided among themselves.

An additional possession, which is valuable in educating future doctors, was her body. Months before she died, she donated her body to the Ohio University College of Osteopathic Medicine. That night, very quickly after she died, her body was taken away to the college.

That was her final good deed. Her gift will allow a future doctor to be taught how to help people.

People treated her well, both in life and in death.

As a very ill patient, she spent time in O'Bleness Hospital in Athens and in Doctors Hospital in Nelsonville. At each hospital, she received excellent care.

Of course, she spent much time at Hickory Creek Nursing Center in The Plains. No one who works there is paid even half what his or her work is worth. In this society, a bad actor in a bad TV series can make hundreds of thousands of dollars a year while the people doing very much more valuable work in nursing homes make very much less money.

Because of my mother, I see the value of such government programs as Social Security, Medicare, and Medicaid. I see how valuable they are in helping provide care for old people. If anything, more money should be poured into these programs and more money should be poured into the government programs that help children. (Healthy adults such as myself should work and pay the taxes that support these programs.)

Of special note is a good deed performed by the Reverend Denver Dodrill. Not being a church-going man—I went to church when my mother went before she began living in nursing homes—I hadn't seen him in two or three years. However, I called him and he came to pray with my mother and read to her Psalm 23, which includes, "Yea, thou I walk through the valley of the shadow of death, I will fear no evil: for thou art with me …."

Many people helped my mother and took care of her and comforted her children. She was much loved—and not just by her children.

Cover Photograph for *Reality is Fabulous: 250 Anecdotes and Stories*:
     Model: Victoria Borodonova
     https://pixabay.com/photos/woman-beauty-fashion-girl-women-5583368/
     https://www.instagram.com/victoriaborodinova/
     https://www.facebook.com/victoria.borodinova

***

This is a short, quick, and easy read.
     Anecdotes are usually short humorous stories. Sometimes they are thought-provoking or informative, not amusing.

***

Educate Yourself
     Read Like A Wolf Eats
     Be Excellent to Each Other
     Books Then, Books Now, Books Forever

***

Do you know a language other than English? If you do, I give you permission to translate this book, copyright your translation, publish or self-publish it, and keep all the royalties for yourself. (Do give me credit, of course, for the original book.)

Chapter 1: From Activism to Clothing

Activism

• In 1993, members of the Barbie Liberation Organization fought against the gender stereotyping of such dolls as Barbie and GI Joe. They bought Barbie and GI Joe dolls and switched their voice boxes and then returned the dolls to the stores. Barbie now said such things as "Troops, attack that Cobra tank at the command post" and "Vengeance is mine," while GI Joe now said such things as "Want to go shopping?" and "I love school, don't you?" and "Will we ever have enough clothes?" Unsuspecting customers bought combat-ready Barbie dolls or effeminate GI Joes. In a comment posted to the Barbie Liberation Organization YouTube video, AnimePRFury wrote, "Man, I wish I had gotten a fixed Barbie! All mine sounded stupid and stereotyped." The Barbie Liberation Organization believes that Barbie wants to learn math and science and wants equal opportunity.[1]

• When British American Tobacco New Zealand set up an official Twitter account, some anti-tobacco New Zealanders asked tough questions: 1) "Do you consider that the thriving marijuana industry poses a threat to cigarettes?" 2) "WHEW! Huf. Huf. I have to go and catch my breath with one of your delicious products. Gasp. Huf. BRB. [Be right back.] Cough." 3) "I quit smoking cos my kids cried that I'd die (like my dad did). How can I smoke without them finding out?" 4) "So, your product is natural, organic and low-fat. You recommend it as a health supplement?" 5) "Do men at tobacco companies have beards — or can they look at themselves in the mirror long enough to shave?"[2]

• Lori Garbacz, a professional golfer, disliked slow play. She once brought a folding chair and a newspaper to the Mazda LPGA Championship to protest the slow play (and to catch up on the news while waiting for her turn to play). At the 1991 U.S. Women's Open, she was so annoyed by the slow play that she went to a pay phone, ordered pizza for herself and her group, and had a pizza party during the tournament.[3]

Actors and Acting

• Michael Caine's shortest audition occurred for a movie that starred Alan Ladd, who was short for a leading man. Mr. Caine walked into the audition and immediately heard "Next!" He asked, "Can't I audition or do something?" The casting agent said, "No, look at your left." To Mr. Caine's left was a mark on the doorway. Anyone who was taller than that mark was immediately rejected for the role. Mr. Caine says, "It was my shortest audition. You had to be shorter than Alan Ladd." Mr. Caine knows what it's like when two actors are mismatched in height. He says, "I did a picture with Elizabeth Taylor, and she stood on a box for the whole movie to be level with me, and for three years everybody thought I was 5-feet-6 because everybody knew how short Elizabeth was." Movie critic Roger Ebert says, "Alan Ladd spent his whole career on a box." When Mr. Ladd made *Boy on a Dolphin* with Sophia Loren, one scene showed them walking on the beach. A trench was dug in the beach, and Ms. Loren had to walk in the trench during the filming of the scene so that she and Mr. Ladd were matched in height.[4]

• At a schools' matinee in 1974, actor Nicol Williamson gave an impressive performance in *Macbeth*. Unfortunately, the chattering of the schoolchildren in the audience annoyed him, so he stepped out of character and told them, "Shut up!" He then said that he could be making a fortune as a motion picture star in America, but that he had chosen to act in a great play by a great playwright in a great theater — so they could d*mn well be quiet while he acted. Furthermore, if the noise continued, he said he would start the play again from the beginning, and he would keep on starting the play from the beginning until he had gotten through it in absolute silence. The schoolchildren kept quiet after his outburst.[5]

• Over 100 years ago, Charles Fechter asked fellow actor Samuel Phelps to appear in *Hamlet*. Mr. Fechter wanted Mr. Phelps to play the Ghost, but he did not make that immediately clear. Mr. Phelps asked, "Who is to play the Prince?" Mr. Fechter replied, "Myself." Mr. Phelps wanted that role for himself, and so he roared at Mr. Fechter, "D*mn your impudence!" The two actors did not appear together in *Hamlet*.[6]

• Jim Backus acted with movie tough guy and star George Raft. He says that Mr. Raft was always a gentleman, always showed up on time, and always knew his lines — and everyone else's. Mr. Backus asked why he was always so professional and why he didn't show up late like a lot of other movie stars and why he memorized the entire script. Mr. Raft explained, "I have to. I don't have any talent."[7]

• When comedian Jack Oakie (who played the Mussolini character in Charlie Chaplin's *Great Dictator*) was pleased with his acting in a movie scene, he used to say, "That was some pretty good pretendin'." Mr. Oakie once saw actor Fredric March wearing the Mr. Hyde makeup for his movie *Dr. Jekyll and Mr. Hyde*. Mr. Oakie asked, "What part are you playing today? I never read the book."[8]

Alcohol

• Monty Python member Graham Chapman was an alcoholic, but for a while even the other members of Monty Python didn't know how bad his problem was because for the most part he was a gentlemanly drunk. However, they learned of the extent of his alcoholism while shooting the sketch "Upper Class Twit of the Year." The Monty Python members needed to check something in a script, but no scripts were readily available, so Michael Palin opened Mr. Chapman's briefcase in search of one. He found a half-empty bottle of vodka and looked stunned. Someone asked him what was the matter, and he replied, "That was full this morning." Mr. Palin found the half-empty bottle at 10:15 a.m. Alcoholism is an undesirable trait for a comedian because he kept forgetting his lines. Once, it took him 24 takes to get his lines right. When he finally succeeded, the studio audience cheered. However, the cheer was unfortunate, because the audience watching the filmed product hears the studio audience cheering, but doesn't know what it is cheering for. Remarkably, Mr. Chapman quit drinking without the aid of Alcoholics Anonymous, and within six months he was in better shape than any of the other members of Monty Python.[9]

• Currently, many people don't want to be thought of as tourists, so if they hear that something is just for tourists, they don't go there. Henry Morgan, however, advises that if you hear that something is just for tourists, then you should definitely go there. Once, Mr. Morgan ran into comedian Eddie Cantor in Paris, and Mr. Cantor asked him what he had done all day. As it turned out, Mr. Morgan had gone to the flea market, taken a trip on the river, lunched in a wine cellar, dined at the Table du Roi, and seen lots of naked chorus girls. This caused Mr. Cantor to sorrowfully admit that he had been to Paris 11 times and all he had seen were "three restaurants and this hotel." While traveling in France, Mr. Morgan went to a vineyard where he saw a workman whose job was to grasp bottles of wine and give them a quarter of a turn. This was the workman's entire job, and he had done it for 31 years.[10]

• William R. Boone was the long-time principal at Orlando High School in Orlando, Florida. He even died on the last day of class ever held at the high school: 6 June 1952. Students then moved to a new high school: William R. Boone High School. Near Orlando High School was Burton's, a bar and grill that students found tempting because it served beer. Jack Caldwell, the 1952 Class President, was with President Boone one day when suddenly President Boone announced, "Let's check out Burton's." They came in through the back door. Students saw Principal Boone and fled through the front door. Principal Boone then told Jack, "That should clear it out for a couple of weeks."[11]

• W.C. Fields was out driving when he picked up a hitchhiker who turned out to be a minister. When the minister saw that Mr. Fields was drinking (his agent was driving), he began to give Mr. Fields a free sermon — a temperance lecture on "The Evils of Alcohol." Mr. Fields told the driver, "Pull up beside the first ditch you see." When the driver stopped, Mr. Fields kicked the minister into the ditch, and then gave him a bottle of gin, with some free advice about how to stay warm in a ditch.[12]

• Mr. Fowler, a Quaker, ran a Temperance Hotel, something that did not always suit his customers. One evening, he saw a chambermaid carrying some hot water — for shaving, she said — to a customer. This made him suspicious, since shaving is usually done in the morning, not the evening. So Mr. Fowler said that he would prepare the hot water for shaving, and he put soap into the container of hot water and — as he had suspected — whiskey.[13]

• American writer Hart Crane once spent three weeks in a Paris prison. He had gone to the Select restaurant, drunk a large amount of Cutty Sark, and then announced that he had no money. Mr. Crane ended up decking four waiters and a police officer before finally being dragged off to prison — with his head banging on the cobblestones of the street.[14]

• Marion Davies once invited teetotaler Calvin Coolidge to one of her parties and deliberately served him sweet wine, telling him that it was fruit juice. Mr. Coolidge liked the beverage so much that he had three servings and told his hostess, "I don't know when I've had anything as refreshing."[15]

Animals

• Like other employees, Walt Disney ate at the concession stand at the Disney Studio. One day, he sat at the counter and ordered just a coffee. A stray dog came in with him, without him noticing, and Mary Flanagan, who ran the concession stand, said, "I'll have to call the guard. I don't know where this dog came from." Walt said, "He's probably hungry. Give him a hamburger." Mary gave the stray dog a hamburger, and then Walt gave her a dollar to pay his bill. Mary gave him 40 cents change, and Walt yelled, "What kind of price are you charging for coffee, Mary?" She replied, "The coffee's only a dime, Walt, but the dog was your guest, and that was 50 cents for the hamburger." Walt laughed. As you would expect, Walt was well loved and had many fans. At the New York World's Fair, teenaged girls came up to him and asked him for his autograph. He signed a few autographs, and then he gently took a girl's hands and said, "Look, honey, I'm going to get mobbed. I can't sign anymore." She screamed, "He touched me! He touched me!"[16]

• A spiritual pretender stayed the night at the house of Mulla Nasrudin, and then tried to impress him by saying: "Last night I left my earthly body and journeyed throughout the cosmos." Nasrudin asked, "When you journeyed throughout the cosmos, did you feel a slight breeze?" "Yes, I did," the pretender said. "Ah," Nasrudin said, "I have bad news for you. Last night, my donkey stuck his tail in your bedroom window, and the breeze you felt was made by the swishing of his tail."[17]

• In April of 1995, Ken Griffey made a bet with Seattle Mariners manager Lou Piniella that he could hit a certain number of home runs during batting practice. Mr. Piniella bet a steak that he couldn't do it. Mr. Griffey lost the bet, and a few days later, when Mr. Piniella walked into his office, he found a 1,200-pound Hereford cow. Mr. Griffey said, "There's your steak."[18]

• Julie Utting of Half Moon Bay, New Zealand, found a great way to make herself feel sexy. In her garden are many tui, which are birds that mimic the sounds they hear. Julie started wolf-whistling at the birds, and now they wolf-whistle at her. Julie says, "It's fantastic — makes my day."[19]

• The *London Metro* has a Good Deed Feed in which people can text short messages thanking people for brightening their day. In June 2012, "Marley The Dog" sent this short message: "Thank you to my wonderful friend for saving me from drowning in the canal."[20]

Authors

• M.F.K. Fisher worked in Hollywood for a while and wrote gags for one of the *Road* movies starring Bob Hope, Bing Crosby, and Dorothy Lamour. She remembers, "The first time I wrote one, my producer said, 'I want you to do a three-minute gag line.'" She wrote it in half an hour and sent it to the producer, who looked at it and said, "This is impossible. Pure plagiarism. Nobody could write this in an half hour." Her business manager told her that she should have taken at least two weeks to write it. Then it would have been accepted. Ms. Fisher began writing at an early age. At age nine, she began writing a novel, and as she finished a chapter she read it out loud to her parents. She stopped writing it because when she read it out loud, her parents kept laughing, although her novel was not meant to be comic. She remembers that she was writing about things she did not understand and that her characters kept "hoping" in and out of bed. Of course, Ms. Fisher understood food and cooking. While she was living in France, her dinner guests did not believe that she had cooked the meal. They thought that she kept the cook hidden so that no one would make the cook a better offer and employ her. Unfortunately, Ms. Fisher never made much money from writing books. In an interview published in 1986, six years before she died, she said that the biggest royalty check she ever got was for $500. Once, she got a royalty check for $10. This did not bother her, she claimed, but it did bother her agent.[21]

• Harry "Steamboat" Johnson was a flamboyant minor-league umpire who wrote and published an autobiography, *Standing the Gaff*. Before games, boys would sell copies of the book to fans in the grandstand. Often, the fans would become angry at Steamboat and throw copies of his book at him. No problem. He simply gathered up the copies of his book and sold them again at the next game.[22]

• A man once plagiarized the work of R' Shmuel Shmelkis, taking the good Rabbi's interpretations and saying they were his. R' Shmuel was unconcerned, saying, "As long as he quotes my interpretations and says they are his, I don't mind at all. I would be concerned if he gave his own interpretations and called them mine."[23]

• The second time that George Plimpton met his first wife, Freddy Medora Espy, she was on a balcony of an apartment in which her hosts were having a cocktail party, and she was looking sadly at the street below. Mr. Plimpton came up behind her and said, "I know a better way down."[24]

Baseball

• On a very hot day in New York, the Pirates were playing the Giants. Frank Frisch, manager of the Pirates, lived in nearby New Rochelle. Neither the Pirates nor the Giants were very good that season, the game was meaningless, and one team got a big lead. At that point, Mr. Frisch came out of the dugout to plead with Mr. Conlan: "I want you to throw me out of this ball game. You know my house up in New Rochelle, Jock. It's a lovely place. It's got trees and green grass and beautiful flowers. And I've got a nice little keg of Schlitz, all iced up, sitting down in the cellar. Jock, this ball club is driving me insane. I can't stand watching these .220 hitters any more. And it's hot. It's too hot. Jock, throw me out of this game. Let me go home." Mr. Conlan replied, "Frank, you're right. It is hot. It's terrible. This isn't much of a ball game. But you're sitting over there in the dugout in the shade next to the water cooler. I'm standing out here in the sun in a dark blue suit, in a mask and shin guards and a chest protector. I'm dying up here. And you're going to die with me. If you think I'm going to throw you out, you're crazy. Go back and suffer."[25]

• In 1981, Los Angeles and Montreal played for the League Championship, and on paper Montreal had the clear edge because of Dodger injuries. The best-of-five series was tied at two games each when Tommy Lasorda gave a pep talk to his players. He said, "Guys, we know we're coming to the end. Montreal seems to be in a better position to win this game and go on to the World Series. I'm proud of all of you. I'm proud of the way we've fought to get this far. I wish I could think of the proper words to express myself, but I can't." After a short pause, Mr. Lasorda continued, "I will simply quote from the Holy Bible, from Romans, Chapter 26, verses 5 through 7 [apparently, his players didn't know that Romans has only 16 chapters]: 'From tribulation comes strength, and from the depths of strength comes character, and from character comes hope.'" Mr. Lasorda then raised his voice and started shouting, "And I hope all of you jack*sses realize that if we don't win this game, we go home!" The Dodgers won in the ninth inning when Rick Monday hit a two-out home run.[26]

• Fans often get on major-league players, managers, and coaches. Usually, the pros ignore the hazing (they are too busy hazing the opposing team to listen), but occasionally a fan will go too far. Once Pittsburgh Pirates manager Danny Murtaugh got up close and personal with a heckler and said to him, "When I was a youngster, I lived on a farm. We had a jackass on that farm that just wouldn't do anything. One day I really gave that jackass a beating. My father heard the jackass hollering and came to his rescue. Then he turned to me and gave me a good lacing for what I had done. His last words were: 'Someday that jackass is going to haunt you.' And you know, up to now I never did believe him." Umpire Beans Reardon was known for cussing right back at players who cussed him. Once the then-President of the National League, Ford Frick, told him that instead of cussing the players, he ought to throw them out of the game. "If I did that," said Mr. Reardon, "I'd have to sit up half the night making up reports. It's easier just to cuss them right back."[27]

• Donald Davidson stood 5-foot-2 (since he was a little person, his business card measured only one inch by two inches) and spent 45 years in professional baseball — as clubhouse boy, publicist, assistant to the president, and traveling secretary. Once, he wore dark glasses and walked through a crowd with the general manager of the Braves, John Quinn. Mr. Davidson was recognized by people in the crowd every few feet, to the amusement of Mr. Quinn, who asked someone, "Tell me, how did you recognize Donald in his dark glasses?" Once, Mr. Davidson asked a couple of baseball players to punch the button for floor 26 in an elevator because he wasn't tall enough to reach that high. They wouldn't do it, so Mr. Davidson rode the elevator down to the lobby, and complained to the manager, "How many times have I told you never to give me a room above the third floor?"[28]

• Lots of stories are told about baseball's Casey Stengel: 1) Back when Casey was managing the Braves, he got a shave in a barbershop after his team had lost both games of a doubleheader. Casey told the barber, "Don't cut my throat — I may want to do that myself later tonight." 2) Casey made a trip to the pitchers mound when Allie Reynolds started to get himself frequently in trouble. Mr. Reynolds made the case that he wanted to stay in the game because he wasn't tired, but Casey said, "You may not be tired, but I am, so I'm taking you out." 3) When he was a baseball manager, Casey once received a telegram from a soldier who criticized his managerial ability. Mr. Stengel wired back, "If you're so smart, let's see you get out of the Army."[29]

• In July 2011, Ian McMillan, age 12, was in the stands watching the Milwaukee Brewers play the Arizona Diamondbacks. In the fourth inning, a player tossed a baseball into the stands, and two boys were close to the ball. Ian got it. (An anonymous adult got the ball first and then gave it to Ian.) Another, younger boy, a Milwaukee Brewers fan, was very disappointed. Ian saw this and gave the baseball to the younger boy. He said later, "It was the right thing to do. I saw the kid. He was really sad." Ian credited his parents with teaching him to do the right thing. ABC caught the good deed on camera, and it appeared on TV. Because of his good deed, Ian was given a baseball bat that his favorite Arizona Diamondbacks player had signed. Ian said, "If you do good things, good things will happen to you."[30]

• Minor-league baseball manager Charlie Frank was always looking for a way to win games. Once, umpire Harry "Steamboat" Johnson was surprised to see a police officer walking out to the pitchers mound in a game when Bob Hasty was pitching. Steamboat called time to investigate the matter, and he discovered that Mr. Frank had taken an injunction out against Mr. Hasty to keep him from pitching! Although the police officer had a warrant for Mr. Hasty's arrest, Steamboat convinced him to wait until after the game to arrest Mr. Hasty by threatening to forfeit the game to the visiting team. Fortunately for Mr. Hasty, he managed to slip out of the baseball park unnoticed, and the arrest warrant was never heard of again.[31]

• The knock-down pitch (aka beanball, brush-back pitch) is a part of major-league baseball. Although pitchers don't often, if ever, throw it to intentionally hurt the batter, they sometimes use this pitch in an attempt to intimidate the batter. In one long-ago game, Kansas City pitcher Virgil Trucks kept shaking off signs from catcher Tim Thompson. Finally, the batter, Red Sox player Billy Klaus, said to the catcher, "Give him the knock-down sign. He wants to knock me in the dust." Mr. Thompson gave the knock-down sign, Mr. Trucks threw the knock-down pitch, Mr. Klaus went down in the dust, and then the duel between pitcher and batter continued.[32]

• In 1936, George Savino played in the major leagues for the first time, and he hit a home run out of the park in his first at-bat for the Baltimore Orioles. Unfortunately, the baseball crashed through a dining-room window onto a table on which a homemaker had just placed her family's dinner. The dinner was scattered everywhere, creating a tremendous mess, and so the homemaker marched over to the baseball stadium to complain. After listening to her, the management liberally reimbursed her.[33]

• Satchel Paige was still pitching at an advanced age, and he heard a lot of jokes about his age. One player asked him, "Satch, what kind of pitch was Connie Mack weak on?" Mr. Paige replied, "That was real funny the first time I heard it — from Abner Doubleday." (Mr. Mack and Mr. Doubleday were early pioneers of baseball; in fact, Mr.

Doubleday invented baseball.) By the way, after Native American athlete Jim Thorpe left an art museum, a reporter asked him, "Which was your favorite work of art?" He replied, *"Custer's Last Stand."*[34]

• Babe Ruth kept late hours and partied but managed to be a terrific ballplayer anyway. Once, Babe came in way after curfew, and Yankees manager Miller Huggins decided that he needed to have a talk with him. The following day, Babe hit two home runs in a game. After the game, road secretary Mark Roth asked Mr. Huggins if he still wanted to talk to Babe, so Mr. Huggins called, "Hi, Babe. How's it going?"[35]

• Baseball great Yogi Berra once was interviewed by Bryant Gumbel, who wanted Yogi to play a word association game with him. Mr. Gumbel said, "Mickey Mantle," and Yogi replied, "What about him?" One day, Mickey and Yogi were discussing the funerals they had been to that year. Yogi said, "Always go to other people's funerals, otherwise they won't go to yours."[36]

• For the most part, umpire Eric Gregg and Dodger manager Tommy Lasorda got along, despite some run-ins. The day after Mr. Gregg had thrown Mr. Lasorda out of a game for arguing too much, Mr. Lasorda kept his back to Mr. Gregg for a while. When Mr. Lasorda finally turned around, Mr. Gregg saw that he had taped his mouth shut.[37]

Children

• In January 2012, a couple, who did not want their names released, headed from Jersey City, New Jersey, on a Path Train bound for St. Luke's Roosevelt Hospital in New York because the woman was beginning to have contractions. Before they could reach the hospital, she gave birth to their first child: a son. He was premature, but he is healthy. The mother said, "I don't think anyone can actually dream of such a delivery." Once they were on the train, the mother quickly discovered that they would not reach the hospital in time for her to give birth there. She said, "I was like, what's going on, I mean something is happening every two minutes, and then I felt, I felt the baby come out." A Good Samaritan, an elderly woman, talked them through the birth process. The father said, "She asked me to check and I checked and then I saw — oh, I can see hair." The couple told the Good Samaritan where they were headed. The father said, "She told me you can't wait that long. The head is out; the baby will choke if you don't take it out." The Port Authority turned the train into an express to get the couple to the hospital as quickly as possible. Meanwhile, the Good Samaritan continued to advise the couple. The father said, "The old lady was always like, do this next, do this next, take it out. Hold the head, take it out." Port Authority Police were waiting at the station. Police officer Atiba Joseph-Cumberbatch said, "We just wanted to make sure the baby was safe, warm, the airways were open." The mother said about her baby, "He has a personality of his own. He decided to come out and that was it. Nothing could stop him." The couple named the boy "Jhatpat," which is Hindu for "fast," which is how he came into this world.[38]

• American food writer M.F.K. Fisher learned about the power of the written word early. Beginning at age seven, she sometimes presented her parents with written pleas and petitions that her parents took seriously. In one plea, she asked that her daily doses of nasty-tasting castor oil be stopped. She also once presented her mother with a petition urging that her mother not bob her hair in the then-current style popularized by dancer Irene Castle. Her sister, the cook, the hired hand, and the iceman also signed the petition. And when she went off to a boarding school, she wrote her father a letter and asked if she could call him Rex. She remembers, "He wrote back and said that all his friends call him Rex. And I was his friend. So, yes, why shouldn't I call him Rex?"[39]

• In 1903, a little girl named Ruth Harding, no relation to President Warren G. Harding, glumly sat for her portrait by the artist Thomas Eakins. In fact, she was so glum that Lady Bird Johnson, looking at the painting along with a group of visitors to the White House, mentioned how grumpy the girl looked. An elderly gentleman among the visitors said that her disposition had improved as an adult, as he knew personally because he was her husband.[40]

• Even as a youngster, Julie Foudy was good in soccer. (In 1996, she won an Olympic gold medal as part of the United States national women's soccer team.) In first grade, she was so good that boys in higher classes asked her to play soccer with them during recess and the lunch period. In the second grade, she wore shorts while the other little girls wore dresses. She also played tackle football with boys, and her brother's friends called her "Jimmy."[41]

• Christians often ask "What Would Jesus Do?" and they try to teach their children to ask the same question. A father noticed his young son's dirty room and asked, "What would Jesus do about cleaning his room?" His son replied, "He'd just pray and zap! — everything would be cleaned up."[42]

• Sometimes, hymn singing can lead to incongruities. William H. Sessions, a collector of Quaker anecdotes, remembers hearing a small, cheerful boy singing, "I should like to die and go to heaven." The incongruity was so striking that Mr. Sessions made faces at the boy to get him to laugh and stop singing.[43]

• When Barry Humphries, who was later a famous Australian comedian, was young, his mother asked him what so many of us ask little children: "What do you want to be when you grew up?" Young Barry replied, "A genius."[44]

• James Isenberg, a Cub Scout chaplain, once asked a number of Cub Scouts to name the Ten Commandments. They immediately started giving examples, including "Don't drink and drive."[45]

• The Reverend Edwin Porter, a Texas preacher, had a grandson who thought that his sermons were the perfect length because they were exactly three comic books long.[46]

Christmas

• Eddie Barefield wanted a C-melody saxophone for Christmas, but his mother got him an alto saxophone and told him, "Santa Claus didn't have any more C-melodies, but he said the alto is going to be very popular so this is the one you should learn." He promptly took it apart so he could see how it was put together. His mother had to take the pieces to a music instrument repair shop so it could be put together again. She found a music teacher who charged 50 cents, and at the first lesson Eddie learned the chromatic scale. He figured that that was all the lessons he needed, so each week he took his mother's 50 cents and went to the movies instead of going for a music lesson. He learned how to play the alto saxophone by listening to and playing along with records. His mother would ask, "Is that your lesson?" And he would reply, "Yes, that's my lesson." As an adult, he played with such jazz notables as Coleman Hawkins, Fletcher Henderson, and Ben Webster.[47]

• When Adlai Stevenson was Governor of Illinois, he went on the offensive against gambling. That Christmas, he had a party at the Governor's Mansion for his children and their friends. The small boys had a room of their own, and they set up a toy roulette wheel and played for pennies. Governor Stevenson observed the toy roulette wheel, and a short time later, a couple of burly police officers "raided" the room and taught the boys a lesson (and gave Governor Stevenson something to laugh about).[48]

Clothing

• In August 1944, the plane of Major Claude Hensinger, a B-29 pilot, and his crew caught fire as they returned from a bombing raid in Japan. They bailed out of the plane. That night, Major Hensinger used his parachute as shelter. In the morning, everybody regrouped, and some friendly Chinese took them to civilization. Major Hensinger kept his parachute. When he proposed to his future wife, Ruth, in 1947, he gave her the parachute so that she could make a wedding dress out of it. Ruth patterned the dress after one in the movie *Gone with the Wind*.

On July 19, 1947, Claude and Ruth were married in the Neffs Lutheran Church in Neffs, Pennsylvania. Their daughter also wore the dress at her wedding and their son's bride wore the dress at their wedding. This dress is now in the Smithsonian in Washington, D.C. The Smithsonian describes the dress in this way: "White; made from parachute; fitted bodice with left side metal zipper; shirred at center front from waist to bust; shirred at side seams at bust; net yoke inset that also forms upper portion of sleeves; opening in yoke at center back, fastened with eight buttons and loops; wide ruffle of lace and net sewn to bottom of yoke; two darts in back bodice; long sleeves; skirt portion of eight panels of parachute; parachute cord in casings placed vertically and drawn up to form poufs; cords pulled up to make skirt shorter in front and create train in back; skirt lightly gathered onto bodice; parachute cord casings, without cords, used as decorative band around bottom of skirt."[49]

• When Angelo Giuseppe Roncalli, a stout man, was elected Pope, he had been a dark horse candidate, and the Vatican tailors were surprised by his election. They had made white soutanes for the leading candidates, but they had not expected that a person of Roncalli's size would be elected Pope. Therefore, the new Pope's first white soutane was very tight. The new Pope, who chose the name John XXIII, joked, "Everybody wanted me to be Pope except the tailors!" (When Pope John XXIII gave his first papal blessing, his clothing was so tight that he could scarcely raise his arms to make the sign of the cross.)[50]

• At one time, Quaker men did not let their facial hair grow because that was regarded as vanity. Some Quakers talked to fellow Quaker Henry T. Humphries because he had a mustache and a beard — one Quaker advised Mr. Humphries, "Put away childish things"! By the way, at one time even the strings of Quaker bonnets were considered worldly, and some Quaker women refused to have strings on their bonnets. One such Quaker woman was Betsy Pike — until the wind blew her bonnet into a river. After that, she wore bonnets with strings.[51]

• Horatio Greenough once created a sculpture of George Washington wearing the costume of a Roman toga. For many years, the sculpture stood outside the Capitol and Mr. Washington's arm pointed toward the Patent Office. Tourists used to joke that Mr. Washington was pointing to the Patent Office because that building contains a display of his uniform, which he wanted to put on.[52]

Chapter 2: From Comedians to Food

Comedians

• Lou Costello of Abbott and Costello fame was a master at getting perks from his movie studio, Universal Pictures. Deanna Durbin was the star actress on the movie production lot, and she had a trailer that served as her dressing room; therefore, Mr. Costello wanted trailers for him and for his partner, Bud Abbott. After making his pitch for the trailers to a Universal executive — and having his request turned down — Mr. Costello said that he would be reasonable, and he would show up for work on time, and he would know his lines. He paused, and then added, "But I don't know how funny I'll be." He and his partner each got a trailer. By the way, Mr. Costello enjoyed gambling, although he lost a lot of money that way. Once, he bet $50,000 on a horse that had a big lead. Mr. Costello turned to a friend, smiled, and then said, "The only way my horse can lose is if it stumbles and falls down." The horse stumbled, fell down — and lost. Also by the way, Mr. Abbott and Mr. Costello once gave the gift of a suitcase to their movie director, Arthur Lubin, a very dignified man. As they gave it to him, the suitcase fell open, and hundreds of condoms fell out.[53]

• Here are some odds and ends about comedians: 1) Stubby Kaye was a fat comedian who played one of the troubadours in the movie *Cat Ballou*. (The other troubadour was Nat King Cole.) He was occasionally billed as an "extra padded attraction." 2) While making *My Little Chickadee* with Mae West, character actress Alison Skipworth became annoyed with the female star and told her, "You forgot I've been an actress for 40 years!" Ms. West replied, "I'll keep your secret." 3) Thirties comic actor Arthur Housman was once asked what was his great ambition in life. He answered, "Oh, to have a chicken farm and a few million dollars." 4) Eddie "Rochester" Anderson was a black man who made it big in Hollywood during the Jim Crow days. Although he played Jack Benny's valet, in real life Mr. Anderson owned a 10-room house and a yacht, and he had two servants of his own. Mr. Anderson was hired by Mr. Benny simply because he was a fine comedian — Jack Benny's valet could have been played by a white man. Rochester didn't get his laughs from playing a black stereotype.[54]

• At the London Palladium, comedian Peter Sellers told the audience that he was a quick-change artist who would show them what Queen Victoria had looked like when she was just a lad. He disappeared for a few moments, then reappeared dressed in unlaced Army boots, a corset, a wig, and a fake beard, while carrying a stuffed crocodile. He then told the audience, "I'd like to be the first to admit that I do not know what Queen Victoria looked like when she was just a lad." By the way, even comedians of genius have to learn their craft before they can demonstrate their genius to audiences. Early in his career, Mr. Sellers bombed so badly that at one point he wheeled a phonograph out on stage, put on a popular recording, and sat and listened as it played. When the record was over, he stood up and took a bow — the audience applauded his sitting down more than they had applauded his act that day.[55]

• While in high school, gay comedian Bob Smith was in the locker room cracking jokes when a fat athlete told him, "God, Smith! You are such a fag!" Mr. Smith replied, "Well, there's a three-letter word that starts with an *F* that describes you, too." He then puffed out his cheeks to make them look fat. By the way, Bob knows a gay couple who named their dogs Lorna, Liza, and Joey — which are the names of Judy Garland's children. Also by the way, Bob is a bird watcher. He is aware that in New York City's Central Park, it's occasionally possible to see parrots flying free that are usually found only in Colombia and Venezuela — they are escapees from Kennedy Airport shipments.[56]

• English comedian Terry-Thomas was telling a funny story in a nightclub once when a heckler shouted "Nuts" right in the middle of the story. Terry-Thomas ignored the heckler and continued telling his story, but at the end of the performance, when he was taking his bows, he asked the waiter, "Have you given that gentleman his nuts?" By the way, born Thomas Terry Hoar Stevens on July 14, 1911, Terry-Thomas choose his stage name from his first two names because he thought they sounded well. But since there was already a famous person in English show business with the last name of Terry, he decided to reverse the names and add a hyphen.[57]

• Comedian Steve Allen had a knack for getting along with everybody. He once hosted a benefit for the NAACP, and told the largely African-American audience, "On this show tonight for the National Association for the Advancement of Colored People, we also have in the audience some Negroes, as well as a few blacks. It's admirable that Negroes, blacks, and colored people can come together and work out their differences." Mr. Allen was once asked, "Do you think it's proper for an unmarried girl to sleep with a man?" he replied, "By no means. She should stay awake all night. You don't know what might happen when you're asleep."[58]

• Colonel Lemuel Q. Stoopnagle was known for his wacky inventions, among them red, white, and blue starch for American flags so they could fly without wind. Another of his inventions was a lighthouse for submarines — it was upside down. Yet another invention was a rowing machine with an outboard motor for people who aren't serious about exercise. He once offered listeners a wonderful prize: the Empire State Building. To get the prize, all you had to do was something very similar to mailing in a boxtop: "Just tear off the top of the Empire State Building, mail it in, and it's yours."[59]

• In the Marx Brothers' Broadway hit *Animal Crackers*, is a scene in which a butler removes Harpo's cape, leaving Harpo only in a T-shirt and undershorts. Once, Harpo didn't put on the undershorts, and when his cape was removed, he was wearing only a G-string. Groucho ad-libbed, "Tomorrow night he's not going to wear anything, so get your tickets early." Apparently, Harpo was the easiest Marx Brother to write for. Marx Brothers writer George S. Kaufman once said, "How can you write for Harpo? All you can say is, 'Harpo enters.' From that point on, he's on his own."[60]

• Groucho Marx was famous for wearing a greasepaint mustache during his theatrical and movie career. (He grew a real mustache for the quiz show *You Bet Your Life*.) When just starting in show business, he wore a paste-on mustache, but once he was late for the show so he used a greasestick to draw a fake mustache. When the owner of the theater demanded the mustache that Groucho usually wore, Groucho picked it up off the dressing table and handed it to him.[61]

• Stand-up comedian Reno can be outrageous. Sometimes in her act she will pretend she is having an orgasm, complete with ear-splitting screams, then say, "At this point, the person you have given your love to could be a radiator for all you care." What does Ms. Reno think about the influence the far right has on the politics of abortion? She says, "Soon a cop will be at the door saying, 'So I hear you had a miscarriage. Prove it.'"[62]

• When Phyllis Diller first started performing comedy, she played in front of Kiwanis clubs, church groups, and sailors at the Alameda Naval Air Station. Once her pay was $17 and a live turkey. Another comedian of an earlier generation (earlier even than Ms. Diller's) was Milton Berle, many of whose jokes really started as ad-libs. He used to hire people to sit in the audience and write down his ad-libs so he could memorize them later and put them in his act.[63]

• Groucho Marx frequently bumped into Sam Goldwyn in Hollywood. Each time, Mr. Goldwyn would ask Groucho how Harpo was doing, but he never asked about Groucho's health. Finally, Groucho got annoyed and protested, "Why do you always ask me how Harpo is? Why don't you ever ask me how I am?" Mr. Goldwyn replied, "I'll do that sometime, Groucho, but right now, how is your brother Harpo?"[64]

• One morning, comedian Jack Oakie was missing from his dressing room; however, he did drive to the movie set and told Charles

Barton, "I won't be working today." When Mr. Barton asked why, Mr. Oakie replied, "It's my birthday," and then drove off. By the way, Mr. Oakie felt that there were three stages to the career of an actor in motion pictures: 1) "Who's he?" 2) "There he is!" and 3) "Is he still around?"[65]

• Radio comedian Henry Morgan was known for making fun of his sponsors. He once claimed that the makers of Life Savers were "mulcting" (swindling) the public because they drilled a hole in the center of their candies. Mr. Morgan offered to take the missing holes and market them as "Morgan's Mint Middles," but his sponsor was not amused and cancelled its sponsorship of his program.[66]

• Comedian Lotus Weinstock says that her name well represents the two sides of her personality. Lotus represents her spiritual side, and Weinstock is the side that busies itself with shopping. One of the messages on her telephone answering machine says, "Lotus is here, but Weinstock is out pursuing her earthly goals. Please leave your number and we'll call back when we are at one."[67]

• Satirist Mort Sahl sometimes performed in dark nightclubs. Like all comedians, sometimes he had to insult a heckler who tried to interrupt his act. Often, Mr. Sahl would tell hecklers, "I guess that's not the first time you've failed in the dark." By the way, Mr. Sahl once said, "I'm for capital punishment. You've got to execute people — how else are they going to learn?"[68]

• Rowan and Martin became very popular on the TV show *Laugh-In* in 1968, with an act that featured Dick Martin as the stupid, funny member of the comedy team. Early in their career, Dan Rowan tried to be the comic, but according to Mr. Rowan, "Dick's one of the worst straight men in the world. He couldn't remember any line unless it was funny."[69]

• Milton Berle was a heterosexual comedian who is famous for dressing in drag. At one of Mr. Berle's parties, actor Jack Lemmon accidentally spilled a drink on himself, so Mrs. Berle told him to go upstairs and put on something of Milton's. When Mr. Lemmon returned to the party, he was wearing one of Milton's dresses.[70]

• TV producer Roger Ailes once watched comedian Mort Sahl sit down and read a newspaper. A few hours later, Mr. Sahl got up on stage and performed 40 minutes of new material — all of which was based on what he had read in the newspaper that afternoon.[71]

• Quaker humorist Tom Mullen has a black friend who tells him that he would look a lot better if he had some color in his cheeks — and in the rest of his body.[72]

Crime

• In May 2012, Danny Lesh of Washington D.C. wrote about someone stealing his bike and putting it up for sale on Craigslist the next day. Mr. Lesh stole his bike back. He had lent his bike to a friend, who had secured it with a cable to her front porch. The next morning the bike had been stolen. She reported the theft to the police and let Mr. Lesh know about the theft. Mr. Lesh said, "It was the first bike I ever bought." In 1998, he had purchased the bike in Chicago. At work the day following the theft, a coworker told Mr. Lesh that a bike matching the description of his bike was for sale on Craigslist. He looked at the ad. He said, "I looked at the pictures. There were stickers that I put on the bike." He called the seller and arranged to meet him. Mr. Lesh took a cab, had it wait out of sight for him, and then approached the seller and asked to take the bike for a test ride. The seller agreed, Mr. Lesh rode around the corner and put the bike in the trunk of the cab, and the cabbie drove him and the bike home. The seller called him later and threatened to report him to the police, but Mr. Lesh filed his own Craigslist post and gave details about the theft of his bike and details about the seller. According to an article in the *DCist* by Benjamin R. Freed, the seller made Craigslist posts about bikes such as "a brand-new Gary Fisher Mamba going for $150. The , a 9-speed mountain bike, normally retails for $989. A discount of more than $800 on a bike that the seller claimed had been used for just two weeks was quite suspicious."[73]

• On a Friday night, a mugger held up Rabbi Shlomo Carlebach. Rabbi Shlomo explained that since it was Shabbos, he was forbidden by his religion to carry money; however, if the mugger would wait until after Shabbos, he could go to Rabbi Carlebach's synagogue and get some money. The mugger did just that; he waited until after Shabbos, went to the synagogue, and Rabbi Carlebach gave him some money, after which the mugger departed.[74]

Critics

• In the mid-1990s, World Championship Wrestling (Ted Turner's outfit) and the World Wrestling Federation warred against each other. The WCW scored major points against the WWF when Alundra Blayze appeared on an WCW program and threw her WWF championship belt into the trash, saying it was worthless. However, the WWF also scored points by having a character named "Billionaire Ted" appear on its programs and act dopey.[75]

• George Moore once said about the novels of Henry James, "Right in front of you, bang, nothing happens." Ben Hecht felt that this comment also applies to television. By the way, Mr. Hecht once said he always had one credo in life: "The boss is always wrong."[76]

• Samuel Johnson was the author of an important English dictionary. To a woman who complained to him about the "dirty" words he had defined in the dictionary, he replied that she must have looked especially for those words.[77]

Death

• A man was sitting beside Solomon in Jerusalem when the Angel of Death came up to him and stared. Immediately, the man fled to China. Later, Solomon asked the Angel of Death why he had stared at the man. The Angel of Death replied, "I am supposed to take that man's soul from him in China, so I was surprised to see him sitting here in Jerusalem."[78]

• Harry Greb was once a middleweight champion in boxing. He used to say, "Here goes nothing," then throw a punch that knocked out his opponent. Lying in bed, dying, his last words were, "Here goes nothing."[79]

Education

• George P. Burdell is one of the most successful student hoaxes ever. In 1927, Georgia Tech accidentally sent two registration forms to Ed Smith, who saw an opportunity and took it. He filled out one form for himself and one for a fictitious student named George P. Burdell. Mr. Smith enrolled Mr. Burdell in the same courses he was taking and even did Mr. Burdell's academic work for him, including writing duplicate tests for himself and for Mr. Burdell. Because of all the work that Mr. Smith did for him, Mr. Burdell graduated from Georgia Tech in 1930 and received a master's degree a few years later. Many stories have been told about Mr. Burdell. The ANAK Society is Georgia Tech's oldest secret society; Mr. Burdell became a member in 1930. Mr. Burdell can be a formidable enemy. When Mr. Burdell was rejected for membership in a fraternity, he ordered a truckload of furniture to be delivered — Cash on Delivery — to that fraternity. Mr. Burdell had an active fictitious career after he graduated from Georgia Tech, although he has continued as an active fictitious student at Georgia Tech throughout his life. Among other things, during World War II, he was on the flight crew of a B-17 bomber that flew 12 missions over Europe. From 1969 to 1981, he served on the Board of Directors of *MAD* magazine. Today, he is on Facebook as a Public Figure, and he has 1,900 followers. In addition, a store named Burdell is in George Tech's student center. Mr. Burdell sometimes signs letters to editors, and he is sometimes paged at football games. In 1969, Georgia Tech computerized registration for its classes. Apparently, Mr. Burdell felt the need to acquire more education because he registered for every course that Georgia Tech offered — over 3,000 credit hours. In 1975 and 1980, he did the same thing. In 2001, he led for a while the online voting for *Time* magazine's Person of the Year Award. Because of Mr. Burdell's great fame, new Georgia Tech students learn his history during orientation. Mr. Burdell does have a personal life. In 1958, the *Atlanta Journal-Constitution* announced the engagement of George P. Burdell and Agnes Scott College student Ramona Cartwright (also a fictitious character). On 23 September 2006, *A Prairie Home Companion* mentioned on the air the 50th wedding anniversary of Mr. and Mrs. George P. Burdell from Atlanta. Today, Mr. Burdell is both an official alumnus of and an active student at Georgia Tech. He is also a Production Assistant on TV's *South Park*.[80]

• Early in his career, tap dancer Gregory Hines used to watch tap master Teddy Hale perform three shows at the Cotton Club. He did one act for the first show, then a completely different act for the second show, and then a third show that was completely different from the first two shows. Mr. Hines marveled and thought, "That's what I want to do. This is it! I don't want to repeat the same routine night after night." Of course, Mr. Hines did learn from masters. He once did a new and very hot step in his act, and the audience loved it and he felt great. About four years later, he saw an old Gene Kelly movie and Mr. Kelly did the exact same step, and Mr. Hines realized that he had seen that movie when he was in his late teens. Of course, although Mr. Hines has developed his own dance style, his dancing shows that he has been influenced by many other dance masters, He says, "I realized it only after watching a video of myself dancing, but I recognized flashes of all my teachers and dance influences."[81]

• Sometimes, it is good to get out of your comfort zone and see the way another cultures does or looks at things: 1) In Asia, monks practice rituals of forgiveness. When meditation teacher U Pandita left after visiting the Insight Meditation Society in Massachusetts, he said, "If I have hurt or harmed you in any way, either intentionally or unintentionally, I ask your forgiveness. And if you have hurt me in any way, either intentionally or unintentionally, I forgive you." 2)

Dipa Ma, a meditation teacher, once suggested to Sharon Salzberg and Joseph Goldstein that they sit in meditation for two straight days. Ms. Salzberg felt that such an effort was beyond her capabilities, but Dipa Ma, a demanding teacher, told her, "Don't be lazy." 3) Some cultures value old people. The Dalai Lama once attended a Buddhist-Christian conference. At the opening ceremony — a tree-planting ceremony — the Dalai Lama noticed a very old monk in a wheelchair. He went to the monk and embraced him, saying joyously, "Oh, he's old!"[82]

• Dancer/choreographer Carmen de Lavallade studied with Lester Horton in a studio at Melrose Avenue in Los Angeles, California. Decades later, she returned to LA and went to visit the old studio. It looked like a souvenir shop, so she walked in and looked for anything that seemed familiar. She remembered the vaulted ceiling, so she looked at it as she walked into the shop. Then her eyes dropped, and she realized that she was a store that sold pornography. She left quickly, but given the history of the place, she considered secretly returning at night to put a commemorative plaque on a wall. Mr. Horton was a generous teacher. When he sent Carmen to study for a while with ballet dancer Carmelita Marracci, he told Carmen, "She can give you what I can't." Carmen says today, "That type of generosity is rarely seen among dance teachers. Between the two of them, I received the most incredible training a young dancer could get."[83]

• Fifth-grader Tyler Sullivan's father, Ryan Sullivan, worked at a Honeywell factory that President Barack Obama visited. No fool, Tyler skipped school so that he could meet the President. President Obama realized that Tyler was missing school, and so on official presidential stationery he wrote for Tyler a note to give to his teacher: "Mr. Ackerman — Please excuse Tyler ... he was with me! Barack Obama." Gawker writer Louis Peitzman wrote this about the note: "Excellent penmanship. Perfectly crafted periods. Proper use of an exclamation point. It works on every level. I also just love how it says 'THE

PRESIDENT' at the bottom [of the official presidential stationery]. Like in case you weren't sure."[84]

• During the Depression, Cornelius Gallagher was worried about losing his job. He was Second Broom (assistant sweeper) at an Electro-Dynamic plant, and he worried that the company might decide that it needed only a First Broom. Therefore, Mr. Gallagher decided to go to college and to study law at night. Later, he became Representative Gallagher (D-NY). According to Mr. Gallagher, if he had been First Broom, he would never have become involved in politics.[85]

• A Buddhist teacher from Thailand once visited the United States and was surprised by Buddhist practices here. Traditionally, generosity is practiced, then morality is taught, and finally there is meditation. But in the United States, people start with meditation, then perhaps study morality, and if they're lucky, a little attention may be given to generosity. The meditation master from Thailand asked, "What's going on here?"[86]

• Marguerite Yingst Parker was one of comedian Richard Pryor's schoolteachers. She came up with an original way to motivate him to attend school. If he attended school on time for a week, she would allow him to perform a school comedy routine in front of his classmates. By the way, Mr. Pryor got a lot of comedic material from his own life. After suffering a heart attack, he joked about the lengths he would go to in order to get new material.[87]

• In 2012, a high school in San Jose, California, had eight female Asian-American students with the last name "Nguyen." The class yearbook allowed students to include a quote, and the eight students, whose photos and quotes were next to one another) arranged their quotes (one or two words per student) to form a message for yearbook readers: "We know / what / you're / thinking, / and / no, / we're / not related!"[88]

• A woman at a subway station was approached by a man who asked about the times the subway ran. Although the woman was holding a subway schedule, she was alarmed because she thought the man looked really weird, so she suggested that he ask another person and pointed to the person he should ask. The man looked at the person and then told her, "Oh! No! I couldn't ask him — he looks really weird!"[89]

• Pope John XXIII spoke several languages fluently, but he had trouble with English. During an audience with President Dwight David Eisenhower, he spoke English only at the beginning and ending of the audience. When President Eisenhower congratulated him on his English, Pope John XXIII replied, "I'm going to night school. But I'm not doing very well. ... I'm always at the bottom of the class."[90]

• A proud mother told Mulla Nasrudin that her son, a recent graduate of a university, had finished his education. Nasrudin smiled, and then he said, "No doubt God will send your son more studies."[91]

Etiquette

• Mulla Nasrudin once went to visit a Very Important Person. He was very happy when he arrived at the VIP's house because he saw the VIP sitting by an upstairs window. However, after knocking on the VIP's door, Nasrudin was informed by a servant that the VIP was out. Nasrudin said, "Please give him my respects, and remind him the next time he goes out not to leave his head by the upstairs window."[92]

• Babe Ruth had little education, especially in etiquette and polite conversation, although he tried to be polite. At an elegant dinner, he was served an asparagus salad, but he pushed his plate away. His hostess asked whether he disliked salad, and Babe replied politely, "Oh, it's not that. It's just that asparagus makes my urine smell."[93]

Fans

• Fame is an odd thing. Before the Winter Olympic Games held in Lake Placid, New York, in 1980, speed skater Eric Heiden, an American, could walk almost anywhere in the United States and not be recognized, but in Norway and the Netherlands, where speed skating is taken seriously, he was constantly recognized and mobbed. Of course, after the publicity generated by coverage of the Olympics, and after he won five gold medals, he started to be recognized and mobbed in the U.S. By the way, in the summer of 1927, Sonja Henie saw Anna Pavlova dance. Immediately afterward, the 14-year-old Sonja began to put ballet moves into her ice-skating routines, and she won gold medals (and fame) at the 1928, 1932, and 1936 Olympic Games.[94]

• Jackie Gleason once took reporter W.J. Weatherby out to dinner. Mr. Weatherby wondered why Mr. Gleason took a cab the very short distance to the restaurant, but he soon found out the reason. As Mr. Gleason walked the few steps from the taxi to the restaurant, several people asked him for his autograph. If he had walked the entire two blocks to the restaurant, he would have attracted a mob. By the way, Mr. Gleason's character of Reggie Van Gleason III was based in part on a rich drunk Mr. Gleason once got mad at for insulting a woman. While walking to Central Park to fight, the rich man said, "Not so fast." Mr. Gleason thought this comment was hilarious.[95]

Food

• One of the more interesting cemeteries in the United States is Ben and Jerry's "Flavor Graveyard," which is located in Waterbury, Vermont. This cemetery has tombstones for discontinued flavors of Ben and Jerry's ice cream, among them "Oh Pear" (1997), "Makin' Whoopie Pie" (2002-2003), and "Urban Jumble" (2000-2001). Standing in the cemetery, Sean Greenwood, Ben and Jerry's Grand Poobah of Publicity, said, "I think we've got the best, and the not-best, up here. Flavors like 'Wild Maine Blueberry.' It's been decades since we made this flavor, but we used to have the trucks back up here with truckloads of blueberries, and everyone would pitch in and unload the blueberries, and make it while the blueberries were fresh." Another example of one of the best discontinued flavors is "Rainforest Crunch," about which Grand Poobah Greenwood recited this poem: "With aching heart and heavy sigh, / we bid Rainforest Crunch goodbye; / that nutty brittle from exotic places / got sticky in between our braces." He added, "You feel bad when the good ones just don't make it anymore." However, Grand Poobah Greenwood said that the "Sugar Plum" ice cream, made of plum and caramel, is a flavor that deserves to be in the cemetery. Visitors enjoy the graveyard. Grand Poobah Greenwood said, "You walk up to the graveyard here, and there'll be fans that are up here putting flowers next to a headstone, or down on one knee, kind of paying their respects."[96]

• Walt Disney's daughter Diane did not name her first child, a boy, after him. He joked that the next baby would be named after him, but the next baby was a girl whom Diane and her husband, Ron Miller, named Tamara. Walt sent a telegram to "Tamara Walter Elias Disney Miller." Diane says, "He was awfully cute." Here's another example of Walt's cuteness: He and imagineer Bob Gurr once visited a coffee shop that had some Disney merchandise on the bottom shelf. Walt preferred that the Disney merchandise be in a better location, and so he began putting it on the top shelf. An employee, not recognizing him, asked, "May I help you?" Walt replied, "No, we're all right. We'll have this done in just a few minutes." By the way, Walt once performed a good deed that went somewhat awry. He and artist Ward Kimball traveled by train to Chicago to see a railroad fair. They went to the dining car and Walt ordered a filet mignon. Ward remembers, "I was looking forward to one of the best dishes I had ever tasted and that was the beef stew, cooked railroad style. They had a way of kind of burning the meat — delicious!" However, when Ward ordered the beef stew, Walt did not think that that was good enough for him, so Walt said, "Beef stew! What do you want that for? Bring him a filet mignon." And so Ward ate a filet mignon.[97]

• Gene Mauch, manager of the Philadelphia Phillies, once got very angry in September of 1964 when a baby-faced rookie named Joe Morgan beat his team by hitting a single in the final inning. After the game, Mr. Mauch went to his team's dressing room and screamed, "WE GOT BEAT BY A GUY WHO LOOKS LIKE A

LITTLE-LEAGUER!" Then he upset the food table in the dressing room, sending potato salad, cold cuts, watermelon, and spare ribs flying everywhere. Everyone was silent for a moment, then a player said, "The food sure goes fast around here."[98]

• Levi-Yitzhak of Berditchev was a friend to the lower classes, the poor, the hungry, the ignorant, the misfits. When other people asked him why, he explained that when the Messiah comes, many people, including kings and patriarchs, would be invited to his feast. As for himself, he would show up at the feast and sit in the last row and hope not to be noticed. But if he should be noticed, and if he should be asked what right he had to be present at the feast, he would ask that mercy be shown to him, because he himself had been merciful to others.[99]

• One of Benjamin Franklin's friends was Thomas Denham, who had borrowed money to start a business in England, failed, and then had gone to America, where he made a fortune. Returning to England, he invited all the people to whom he owed money to a dinner. None of the people had ever expected to be paid, so they were happily surprised at the end of the dinner to find the money they were owed, plus interest, under their plates.[100]

• Benjamin Franklin tried to be a vegetarian, but he was unsuccessful at it. Once, his host fried fish, and the smell of the fish was very appetizing. Mr. Franklin thought about whether he should eat the fish or remain true to his principles, but when the fish's stomach was opened up and some smaller fish taken out, he thought, "If you eat one another, I don't see why we mayn't eat you." Mr. Franklin greatly enjoyed his dinner of fish.[101]

• Nancy Nesbitt was the White House cook at the beginning of Harry Truman's Presidency, but she wasn't a good one. President Truman mentioned to her that he didn't like Brussels sprouts, but she served Brussels sprouts to him three days in a row. Not surprisingly, the new no-nonsense President fired the long-time White House cook.[102]

• In 1995, the Bio Café opened at MIT's then-new biology building. Students quickly hacked (pranked) it, setting up their own Biohazard Café on spring registration day. On the menu were Humungous Fungus Pizza, Soylent Green, and Lab Mice on Rice. Before consumption, however, the diner had to sign a release form.[103]

• Mulla Nasrudin had some fine seven-year-old vinegar. One day, a distant relative knocked on his door and asked for some of the vinegar. Nasrudin declined, saying, "If I were to let all my distant relatives have some of my vinegar, it wouldn't last for seven days, let alone seven years."[104]

Chapter 3: From Free Speech to Money

Free Speech

• Barry Took, the man who first proposed the teaming up of six comedians into the comedy troupe Monty Python's Flying Circus, took their side in the battle against censorship. After Monty Python started working on their TV series, the head of BBC Light Entertainment, Tom Sloane, said to Mr. Took, "Excuse me, Barry, I've just been looking at a playback of *Python*. Does John Cleese have to say 'bastard' *twice*?" Mr. Took replied, "Yeah, if he wants to." No more discussion took place, and the word appeared twice in the sketch.[105]

• Zero Mostel and Jack Gilford were both victims of the blacklist in the Joe McCarthy era. When they were getting ready to star in *A Funny Thing Happened on the Way to the Forum*, Jerome Robbins, who had been a friendly witness before the House UnAmerican Activities Committee, was called in as a script doctor. Both Mr. Mostel and Mr. Gilford were professionals, so they did not object (despite some soul-searching by Mr. Gilford). As Mr. Mostel pointed out, "We of the left do not blacklist."[106]

Friends

• Bob Dole considered the late Teddy Kennedy a friend. Mr. Kennedy's mother was born on July 22, and on the first July 22 after she died, Mr. Dole sent Mr. Kennedy a note saying that he was thinking of him and her. Mr. Kennedy wrote back that if his mother were still alive, she would wish him luck in the Presidential election — but not too much luck.[107]

• A blind woman needed to attend a meeting, and a friend offered to drive her there. The blind woman gratefully accepted the offer, then joked, "Remember, if you arrive and all the lights are out, that doesn't mean I've already left."[108]

Gays and Lesbians

• When gay comedian Bob Smith broke up with his long-time boyfriend, Tom, his mother complained, "The neighbors were just getting used to the idea of me talking about Bob having a boyfriend. I don't think they're going to like me talking about him having several boyfriends." Other tragedies occurred. During retirement, Bob father drank so much that it endangered his health. Bob's brother suggested an intervention, but his sister asked, "Who would we get to intervene? Dad drinks with everyone in town." By the way, Bob is aware that in West Hollywood is a coffeehouse named the Weho Lounge that has these signs hanging out front: "Lunch Specials" and "Free HIV Testing." Also by the way, Bob speculates that the real reason the rich find it difficult to enter Heaven is because they have to use the servant entrance.[109]

• Lots of people wonder how one becomes a homosexual. According to lesbian comic Suzanne Westenhoefer, the would-be homosexual must pass a talent competition, an evening-wear competition, and the all-important swimsuit competition. By the way, some people believe that God used AIDS to punish homosexuals, even though heterosexual women and babies get AIDS — and lesbians do not. However, according to lesbian humorist Ellen Orleans, "AIDS is God's way of testing straight people for compassion and intelligence in dealing with a pandemic disease. So far, society isn't doing too well."[110]

• Lesbian performance artist Holly Hughes says that her hobby is "chasing girls (who don't look like girls)." She also remembers her favorite show (right in the front row, Raquel Welch was sitting) and her most terrifying show (right in the middle, Raquel Welch walked out). By the way, another performance artist, Tim Miller, counts among the "honors" he has received his arrest record with Act Up, an activist group on behalf of gay and lesbian issues.[111]

• The off-Broadway show *Family Secrets*, written by Sherry Glaser and her husband, Greg Howells, contains a scene in which a father confronts his lesbian daughter. She asks whether it's normal to love someone, and he replies, "Not a woman." She then says, "You love Mom."[112]

Gifts

• When Ken Kettlewell, author of *Presidential Passages*, a book about the Bibles the Presidents of the United States used at their inaugurations, was 12 years old in 1937, one of his teachers, Paul M. Davis, invited him to listen on his radio to the third inaugural address of Franklin Delano Roosevelt. Mrs. Davis served cookies, and in his book Mr. Kettlewell writes, "I don't remember the inaugural address. I do remember the cookies." By the way, the Bible that Grover Cleveland used at both of his inaugurations was a gift. Clerk of the Supreme Court James H. McKenney reported, "He was the owner of a small Bible, not larger than our hand. His mother had presented it to him when he was a boy, and he had treasured it ever since. It was used at both Inaugurals." The Bible on which Calvin Coolidge took the oath of office was given to him when he was a boy by his grandmother. While staying at his father's house, Vice President Coolidge received a telegram at midnight telling him that President Warren G. Harding had died. Mr. Coolidge's father, who had been asleep, got up and administered to his son the oath of office.[113]

• Gaylord Perry was known for throwing the spitball. When he was traded by the New York Giants to the Cleveland Indians, some friends gave him a party. Umpire Chris Pelekoudas was the head speaker, and at the end of his speech, he gave Mr. Perry a going-away present: a five-pound jar of Vaseline.[114]

• Final gifts are often the most important. On his deathbed, an old man made his son promise to sit — alone — for a half hour every day in the best room.[115]

Golf

• Playing at the Master's Tournament is the dream of all golf players. After playing at the 1995 Master's — his first — Tiger Woods sent this note to the Master's officials: "Please accept my sincere thanks for providing me the opportunity to experience the most wonderful week of my life. It was fantasyland and Disney World wrapped into one. … it was here that I left my youth behind and became a man." By the way, Tiger is one-quarter black, one-quarter Thai, one-quarter Chinese, one-eighth Native American, and one-eighth Caucasian. Because he is a member of several minorities, he received a death threat when he played in his first professional tournament. When he won the 1997 Master's Tournament, no other player had — or needed — security guards, but Tiger was under the protection of six security guards. After winning the 1997 Master's Tournament, Tiger was given the traditional green coat worn by winners by Nick Faldo, who had won in 1996. Referring to Tiger's African heritage, his father, Earl, told him, "Black and green go well together, don't they?" By the way, before Tiger was two years old, his father took him to the golf course to play with sawn-off clubs. Soon after, Tiger appeared on television, where he defeated comedian Bob Hope in a putting contest.[116]

• Although he was a professional golfer, Bruce Lietzke was not averse to taking it easy for long periods of time. After playing in the 1985 Texas Open, Mr. Lietzke told his caddy to be sure to clean the clubs very well because he was going to skip the U.S. Open and wouldn't play golf again until the Bob Hope tournament, a couple of months off. His caddy didn't believe that Mr. Lietzke was going to stop playing golf for that long — after all, wouldn't he have to practice? — so he stuck a banana in the driver headcover. A couple of months later, the caddy prepared Mr. Lietzke's clubs for the Bob Hope tournament — and found a rotten banana in the driver headcover.[117]

• Harry Vardon was an immensely talented golfer. Once, he hit an excellent shot near the hole, and someone watching him exclaimed, "What a lucky shot that was!" Mr. Vardon didn't say anything, but he hit 12 more balls from the same spot, and all 12 balls landed near the hole. By the way, Walter Hagen was such a graceful winner that sometimes the person he had just beaten would carry Mr. Hagen's clubs back to the locker room.[118]

• Professional golfer Carolyn Hill accidentally left her putter behind at a water cooler after slaking her thirst during the 1982 United States Women's Open Championship. Needing to putt, she sent her caddie back to retrieve her putter, but rather than holding up play, she successfully putted the ball using her driver. The caddie returned, and Ms. Hill, preparing to hit a drive, requested of the caddie, "My putter, please."[119]

• Golfer Jack Nicklaus had remarkable powers of concentration. Once, he was in a play-off against Arnold Palmer, whose Army buddies were very vociferous in their support of Mr. Palmer and who yelled, "Miss it, Fat Jack," whenever Mr. Nicklaus prepared to putt. After Mr. Nicklaus had won the play-off, he was asked if the crowd had bothered him. He replied, "Crowd? What crowd?"[120]

Good Deeds

• In May 2012, Gabby Smart, a 12-year-old girl who lives in Clinton, Montana, asked for horse supplies for her birthday. The horse supplies weren't for her; they were for Bitterroot Valley's Willing Servants, a horse-rescue charity. Gabby and her mother, Nicole, were able to deliver a pickup load of horse supplies to Willing Servants. Nicole said, "We're very blessed as a family. We've always tried to do what we can to help others." When Gabby was eight years old, she and her mother talked about doing good deeds. Gabby said, "My mom and I were talking about ways that children could give back. I thought maybe it would be a good idea to donate my presents. I decided right then I would do that every other year." When she was nine years old, her friends at her birthday party bought her leashes and collars and other small-animal stuff that she donated to the Missoula, Montana, animal shelter. Gabby said, "They were all so happy. It made me feel good. It was nice to feel like I'm doing something to help. It made me want to do it some more." Willing Servants founder Theresa Manzella said, "It really just blows me away that an eight-year-old can come up with an idea like this. We're all called to be cheerful givers. For me, it's an honor that she selected us." Gabby said, "Birthdays aren't really about getting a bunch of stuff, you know. It's supposed to be a celebration of another year. I like to do something that's not all about you. I think we should spread our thankfulness. This is actually really fun. It's so nice to be able to give it all away to someone who really needs it. If kids just knew how good it makes you feel, maybe more might start doing this, too. Can you imagine how that would make people feel? I think it could really help."[121]

• In July 2012, Sam Nagy of Huddersfield, West Yorkshire, England, had an operation to remove one of his kidneys so it could be transplanted into a complete stranger. Mr. Nagy is a 20-year-old banking administrator, the youngest altruistic organ donor in Great Britain. Some people thought that he was too young to make such an important decision, but he said, "By the time I had done all the research ... I thought, 'I am quite mature for my age, what difference is a few years going to make?' If there are people on the waiting list who are in quite a bad way ... what is the reason for waiting a few years?" His mother, Karen, was worried about the operation. She said, "I'm extremely proud of him, but part of me thinks, 'At what point in your life as a young man do you wake up and think that this is what you want to do?'" Mr. Nagy has a blog titled "Altruistic Donation, My Journey to Save A Life," on which he wrote, "I'm just an average person, no amazing talents, no special abilities, just a motive to help."[122]

• Roger Clayton, from Paignton, Devon, England, found a parking ticket on his car when he went seven minutes past his allotted time for parking. Since then, he has been doing such things as putting 50 pence into parking meters when he notices that they are nearing their expiration time for parking. He said, "I saw a traffic warden standing with his machine at Paignton beach, so I went over and noticed the car's ticket was about to run out. So I just bought another ticket, put it under the car's windscreen wiper and walked away." He added, "I felt good — we all work hard — if you've only got 50p to put in a meter or you get stuck in a queue it's not really your fault you overrun your time. It happened to me on a Sunday afternoon. I nipped in a shop with my son to buy a pair of shorts and when I came back I had a fine."[123]

Hunting

• One day, Mulla Nasrudin went bear hunting. When he returned from his hunting trip, a friend asked him how the trip had gone. Nasrudin replied, "Perfect." The friend then asked how many bears Nasrudin had shot, but Nasrudin replied, "None." Next, the friend asked how many bears Nasrudin had seen, and Nasrudin again replied, "None." So the friend said, "You said that you had a perfect bear-hunting expedition, and yet you didn't see any bears. How can you say that the bear-hunting expedition was perfect?" Nasrudin replied, "When you are hunting for dangerous animals such as bears, 'none' is the perfect number of bears to see."[124]

• In 1861, some Quakers were considering the question of whether anyone in the Meeting was guilty of pursuing "Vain Sports or Amusements." The Clerk of the Meeting, Nathaniel Morgan, turned to Thomas Trusted, a Quaker who was very fond of partridge hunting, and asked if he were guilty. Mr. Trusted replied, "No, 'tain't the season," so all the Friends at the Meeting were innocent of this particular trespass.[125]

Husbands and Wives

• In 1971, Margaret Trudeau married Canadian Prime Minister Pierre Trudeau. She was much younger — and wilder — than he. Marijuana smoke often could be smelled outside her window in the Prime Minister's residence in Ottawa. A police officer even once gave her a bag of incense so she could disguise or cover up the smell. Of course, because she was the wife of the Prime Minister and a flamboyant personality, people, including people in the media, paid attention to her. Supposedly, she once consulted a psychiatrist about what she thought was her paranoia, but the psychiatrist told her, "Everybody *is* watching you. That's not paranoia. That's reality."[126]

• Ida M. Pardue was issuing a marriage license to a couple one day when the woman suddenly grew angry, telling her boyfriend, "You told me this was your first marriage!" Her boyfriend was shocked and said it was his first marriage, so the woman showed him that he had written "2" where the license application form said, "Number of marriages." "Oh," said her boyfriend, "I thought that meant how many people were getting married."[127]

• Following a church sermon about Joseph, a small boy had some questions for his mother. Asked what a spouse is, the mother replied, "A spouse is somebody's husband or wife." Asked what a "most chaste spouse" is, the mother replied, "That means St. Joseph was a good, pure, and holy husband. What do you think it means?" The boy replied, "I think it means that all the women were after him, but Mary got him in the end."[128]

• James Joyce's wife, Nora, read Molly Bloom's soliloquy (which was largely responsible for getting the novel banned) in his controversial novel *Ulysses*. After reading it, she told Robert McAlmon about her husband, "I guess the man's a genius, but what a dirty mind he has, hasn't he?" By the way, Mr. Joyce wanted to read Henrik Ibsen in the original, so he studied Norwegian while at Dublin's University College.[129]

Illnesses and Injuries

• Baseball great Yogi Berra came home from the ballpark early one afternoon to find his wife and son Tim gone. When they returned, he asked where they had been. Carmen, his wife, replied, "I took Tim to see *Doctor Zhivago*." Mr. Berra asked, "What the h*ll's wrong with him now?" By the way, while Mr. Berra was advertising Yoo-Hoo soft drinks, his son Larry played on the Montclair High School basketball team. Whenever the team won, Mr. Berra delivered lots of Yoo-Hoo to the locker room, but whenever the team lost, Mr. Berra would say, "If you win, you get the Yoo-Hoo; if you lose, you get the Boo-Ooo!"[130]

• After having a mastectomy, comedian Danitra Vance (1959-1994) went on stage and performed as the character Harriet Hetero the Feminist Stripper. At one point in her act, she stripped off her shirt to reveal one breast. Over the place where her other breast had been was a taped X. Why did she do this? She answered, "I had to show that this body is okay." By the way, Ms. Vance studied anthropology at Roosevelt University in Chicago. A teacher wanted her to go to Haiti and study the culture there, but she replied, "I want to study cultures like Los Angeles."[131]

• Marty Ingels was married to actress/singer Shirley Jones and was a good comedian who starred in the TV sitcom *I'm Dickens — He's Fenster*. Unfortunately, through much of his career he suffered from panic attacks. Once, he stayed in his apartment for nine months, afraid to go out into the open air. He also once picked up his date for the evening — Shirley Jones — in a motor home so he technically wouldn't have to leave his home.[132]

• Lesbian comedians Robin Tyler and Patty Harrison used to do a routine about faith-healer Brother Ripoff. As Brother Ripoff, Ms. Tyler would say to Ms. Harrison, who was playing an ill lesbian looking for healing, "This woman's come to me and she's a lesbian and she wants to be healed. I'm going to put my hand on her and I'm going to heal her. Hallelujah! You are now healed — and you're still a lesbian!"[133]

Language

• In World War II, the troops of General Joe Stilwell were driven back by Japanese troops in Burma. When General Stilwell heard that the defeat was being described as a "tactical retreat," he said firmly, "I claim that we took a h*ll of a beating."[134]

• Before a football game, Yale telegraphed Harvard, "May the best team win." Harvard telegraphed back, "May the better team win."[135]

Mishaps

• Richard Dennis appeared in the play *Murder by Death*. At the end of Act II, his character was punched in the jaw, so each night he secreted a pouch of stage blood in his mouth so that during the fight scene he could let a trickle of blood run down his chin. Unfortunately, one night he accidentally bit into the pouch too early, and he was forced to cover up the accident by apologizing to the other characters about his bleeding gums.[136]

• The Grant food chain once attempted to create a hot dog without cancer-causing nitrates. It sent a package of the healthy hot dogs to the United States Department of Agriculture so they could be tested, but an official there thought that they were a gift, so he took them home and had a weenie roast.[137]

• Dancing in an open-air theater has its challenges — bats, for example. Another danger is picnickers. Tanaquil Le Clercq once danced an adagio in an open-air theater in Colorado with a hot-dog wrapper made sticky with mustard clinging to her tights.[138]

Money

• While the Marx Brothers were in London, Groucho's son, Arthur, used to kick a soccer ball in Hyde Park until a Bobby told him and Groucho that the park was the "Queen's grazing ground" and sports weren't allowed. Groucho protested, "The Queen's grazing ground! What's the matter with the food at Buckingham Palace that she has to come out here and eat grass?" Late in Groucho's life, the Queen asked him to do a one-man show for her. He was pleased by the compliment and considered doing the show — until he found out that by tradition the proceeds would be donated to charity. He responded to the invitation, "Tell the Queen that Groucho doesn't work for nothing."[139]

• Back in the 1950s, much pro wrestling was controlled by the National Wrestling Alliance (NWA), which carefully determined who would be its champion. Annually, the promoters of the NWA met to decide whether the current champion would stay champion or lose to someone new during the following year. Whoever was champion was required to post a bond of several thousand dollars to ensure that he followed orders and won or lost according to the direction of the promoters. The money was returned to the champion only after he lost to the wrestler the promoters told him to lose to.[140]

• While making *The Hustler* with Paul Newman, Jackie Gleason challenged Mr. Newman to a game of pool. To make it interesting, they made a bet. Mr. Gleason ran 50 straight balls, and Mr. Newman owed him $50. The next day Mr. Newman paid his debt — with 5,000 pennies. By the way, while Mr. Gleason was in the hospital in an attempt to lose weight, the writers of *The Honeymooners* decided to see him to get his input on a script. However, when they arrived at the hospital, a nurse told them, "Mr. Gleason has gone home. He said he wasn't feeling well."[141]

• A caddy at the Royal and Ancient Golf Club at St. Andrews in Scotland once received a three-penny tip. Even though this happened a long time ago, three pennies was *not* a good tip. The caddy looked at the three pennies, then told the golfer he had caddied for that he could tell his fortune from the three pennies. Then he explained that he learned from the first penny, "Yer no' a Scotsman." The second penny told him, "Yer no' married." Finally, the caddy said, "The third one tells me that yer father wasn't married either."[142]

• When soccer superstar Julie Foudy was ready to attend college, she had scholarship offers from several universities, including Stanford and North Carolina. Stanford was expensive — $20,000 a year — and Ms. Foudy was offered only a partial scholarship of $2,000 a year to go there. North Carolina was much less expensive. In fact, when the North Carolina coach visited her, he said, "How would you like for us to save you $80,000?" (Ms. Foudy ended up going to and graduating from Stanford anyway.)[143]

• Anna Galina, a wealthy woman, was the student of Tatiana Piankova, who had danced with Anna Pavlova and her company. A

French newspaper once printed as fact that Ms. Piankova had never danced with Ms. Pavlova. Ms. Galina sued the newspaper, won, and was given a check by the newspaper. She tore the check up, but told the newspaper to apologize in print for its error. The newspaper did print the apology, and Ms. Galina never again danced in France.[144]

• Chi Chi Rodriguez once came to Sam Snead for help with his golf swing. Mr. Snead asked him, "Chi Chi, you know how you hit the ball and almost fall down? You're falling down now before you even hit the ball." Chi Chi listened to the advice, then told Mr. Snead, "If I win, you get $5,000." Chi Chi did win — $350,000 — and he sent Mr. Snead's check to him. (The caddie who delivered the check told Mr. Snead, "Don't cash it for a week.")[145]

• Zero Mostel considered Cézanne's *Mont St. Victoire* to be a master work of art — "a fantastic wonder to behold." According to Mr. Mostel, "That painting is one of the highest aspirations of man in our history. Would you believe that I have heard people say it's overpriced, at $750,000? Yet nobody says that about the billions we spend for bombs. I wish I could reverse the values. Less dreadnoughts, more painting."[146]

• Zeppo Marx realized that he was the least funny of the Marx Brothers, and he soon stopped his movie career in order to become a very successful agent. After Zeppo quit, someone asked the Marx Brothers if they would start accepting less money because there were now three Marx Brothers instead of four. They answered, "What do you mean? Why, we're twice as good without Zeppo."[147]

• Many churches have trouble raising funds. Rev. Steve W. Caraway, who is the pastor of University United Methodist Church in Lake Charles, Louisiana, once reported to his congregation: "I have good news and bad news about our pledges. The good news is: we have reached our goal. The bad news is: you still have them in your pocket."[148]

• During World War II, Spike Milligan had a torrid affair with a W.A.A.F. Corporal named Bette. After he was shipped to fight overseas, she wrote him red-hot letters. To raise money, Mr. Milligan used to auction them off to the lechers in his outfit.[149]

Chapter 4: From Movies to Revenge

Movies

• Victor Mature and Jim Backus acted together, and they were cadets at military school together. Neither did well at military school; both succeeded in infuriating the Colonel in charge of the military school. The Colonel even bawled them out, told them to stay out of his sight, and predicted that they would end up as gutter bums. A few years later, Mr. Mature and Mr. Backus were successful movie actors. One day, they were making a movie together, and Mr. Mature got an idea. The movie set was a penthouse, and Mr. Mature, Mr. Backus, two starlets, and not much feminine clothing posed together on the set for a photograph that Mr. Mature sent to the Colonel with this note: "Best wishes from Cadets Mature and Backus. P.S. How are your honor students doing?"[150]

• Harpo Marx once appeared in a silent film without his famous brothers. The year was 1925, and the movie was *Too Many Kisses*. Harpo was very excited about being in a movie and invited all his friends and family members to come with him and see the movie. Unfortunately, most of Harpo's appearance ended up on the cutting room floor. Everyone kept waiting for Harpo to appear in the film, and finally there was a shot of him. "There he — " his mother started to say, but the shot was over before she finished her sentence. Unfortunately, Harpo had dropped his hat on the floor and was bending over to pick it up during the shot, so he never did see himself on screen.[151]

• In 1975, Clint Eastwood directed and starred in *The Eiger Sanction*. In one scene of the movie, his character dangles from a wire thousands of feet up in the air while mountain climbing. Mr. Eastwood told film critic Roger Ebert, "I didn't want to use a stunt man because I wanted to use a telephoto lens and zoom in slowly all the way to my face — so you could see it was really me. I put on a little disguise and slipped into a sneak preview of the film to see how people liked it.

When I was hanging up there in the air, the woman in front of me said to her friend, 'Gee, I wonder how they did that?' and her friend said, 'Special effects.'"[152]

• At one time, movies were advertised differently on the marquees of theaters in black neighborhoods than on the marquees of theaters in white neighborhoods. Judging by the marquees of theaters advertising Hollywood movies in black neighborhoods, blacks were often the stars, instead of supporting actors. For example, marquees would say such things as "Bill Robinson in *The Little Colonel*," "Canada Lee in *Lifeboat*," "Hattie McDaniel and Butterfly McQueen in *Gone with the Wind*," and "Dooley Wilson in *Casablanca*."[153]

Music

• Eddie "Lockjaw" Davis became a musician not because of a love of music, but because he watched musicians and he noticed that they drank, they smoked, they got women, and they slept late. He watched to see which musicians were most noticed, and he noticed that the drummers and the tenor saxophonists were widely noticed. To him, playing the drums looked like it took more work and so he learned to play the tenor saxophone. When he told this story, he always said, "That's the truth." He probably made a good decision not to play the drums. Lester Young played drums, but he switched to the saxophone because he would want to spend time with a woman, but while he was busy putting away his drums after a gig her mother would call her and she would leave and go home. Putting away a saxophone was a whole lot quicker.[154]

• James J. Walker (1881-1946) was famous both as the mayor of New York City and as the composer of the song "Will You Love Me in December as You Do in May?" At his funeral, the organist intermingled "Here Comes the Bride" with "Will You Love Me in December as You Do in May?" This confused a couple of Mr. Walker's friends: ex-fighter Mike O'Toole and "Rubbernose" Kennedy. Finally, they figured out what must be happening — because the funeral was taking place in a church, the organist must be playing "Will You Love Me in December as You Do in May?" in Latin.[155]

Names

• Olympic gold-medal gymnast Mary Lou Retton has a short, powerful build that can become stocky if she doesn't watch what she eats. Her family's original, Italian name was "Rotundo," which means round, and her coach Bela Karolyi often called her by the nickname "Booboolina," which means fat. By the way, she is 57 inches tall, and her competitive weight was 94 pounds. Also by the way, her world-class gymnastics coach, Bela Karolyi, defected from Romania to the United States. After defecting, Mr. Karolyi went to Immigration to fill out forms for political asylum. While he was there, a Vietnamese man also with forms to fill out grabbed his sleeve to indicate that he wanted his help. Mr. Karolyi told him in Romanian, "What do you want, comrade? I don't speak English. I am just like you. I can't even fill my own forms out."[156]

• "Hole-in-'is-pocket," a caddie of the Royal and Ancient Golf Club at St. Andrews in Scotland, got his nickname because during money matches, the golfer he was caddying for would sometimes make a bad shot and lose his ball, but "Hole-in-'is-pocket" would let a ball drop down his trouser leg and say, "Here it is, sir, an' no' such a bad lie after all." Another caddie of the Royal and Ancient Golf Club at St. Andrews in Scotland, got his nickname "Stumpie Eye" because he was half blind. He used to tell the golfers he caddied for, "I can carry clubs all day, sir, but ye'll have to watch the ball for yourself." By the way, a century ago, many golfers gave their clubs names. For example, Allan Robertson gave these names to some of his clubs: "The Doctor," "Sir Robert Peel," and "The Frying Pan."[157]

• Here are some stories about names: 1) Theatrical actress Beatrice Lillie was married to Sir Robert Peel, one of whose ancestors (with the same name) organized the Metropolitan police force of London. In recognition of this ancestor, London police officers are known as

"Bobbies." 2) Eve Arden was born Eunice Quedens. She got her stage name by combining the name of the first woman in the Bible, which she was reading when she decided she needed a stage name, with the last name of famous cosmetics queen Elizabeth Arden. 3) Comedian Judy Holiday starred in such classic comedies as *Born Yesterday* and *The Solid Gold Cadillac*. Her real name was Judith Tuvim — "tuvim" is Hebrew for holiday.[158]

• Here are two stories about names: 1) When Shirley Shrift changed her name to Shelley Winters, a friend named Josh Shelley told her, "Well, that does it. We can't get married. That would make you Shelley Shelley." 2) Actor Jack Gilford had trouble with reporters misspelling his name as "Guilford." He once wrote a letter of complaint to columnist Earl Wilson and began the letter, "Dear Mr. Wuilson."[159]

• One of King Charles II's mistresses was the actress Nell Gwyn, who bore him at least one son. After the illegitimate son was born, she was distressed because he had no title, so she stood on a balcony and threatened to throw him off. King Charles II, who was riding a horse, knew what the problem was, so as he galloped past the balcony, he shouted out, "Spare the Earl of Burford."[160]

• Babe Ruth was terrible at remembering names, and he was sometimes terrible at remembering faces. Miles Thomas had been a Yankees pitcher for three or four years, but one day someone decided to have some fun and introduced Mr. Thomas to Babe as a new Yankee pitcher. Babe told Mr. Thomas, "Nice to see you, kid. Welcome to the Yankees."[161]

Politics

• On October 19, 1932, Franklin D. Roosevelt had made a speech in Pittsburgh in which he promised to reduce government spending, but of course as President he greatly increased government spending. In his 1936 election campaign President Roosevelt was plagued by the use his political opponents were making of the speech, so he gave a copy of the speech to a ghostwriter, Judge Rosenman, and asked him to write a new speech "explaining" the old speech. However, after examining the old speech, Judge Rosenman told President Roosevelt, "Mr. President, the only thing you can say about that 1932 speech is to deny categorically that you ever made it."[162]

• John F. Kennedy defeated Republican Richard Nixon by only 50,000 votes. Shortly after the election, President Kennedy read an article that praised one of his aides as being "coruscatingly" brilliant. Mr. Kennedy remarked, "Those guys should never forget, 50,000 votes the other way and we'd all be coruscatingly stupid." By the way, in 1961, President Kennedy met a pessimistic businessman. Trying to cheer up the businessman, President Kennedy said, "Why, if I weren't president, I'd be buying stock." Not impressed, the businessman said, "If you weren't president, so would I."[163]

• This is an underground joke: Because of business, a man once went to live in Soviet Russia. Because there was censorship, he knew that he would have to praise Soviet Russia if he wanted his letters to be delivered. Therefore, he agreed with a friend that if conditions were good in Soviet Russia, he would write in blue ink, but if conditions were bad he would write in red ink. A few weeks passed, and a letter arrived. It was written in blue ink and praised Soviet Russia, but at the end was a note: "I would have written in red ink, but it's impossible to get any here."[164]

• At the Constitutional Convention, when our founding fathers got together to create the Constitution of the United States, Benjamin Franklin was very helpful in persuading people to compromise when necessary. When disagreements threatened to get completely out of hand, Mr. Franklin told the story of a little French girl who marveled that out of all the many people in the world, she was the only person who was always right.[165]

• Even after the Declaration of Independence was adopted on July 4, 1776, many American colonists still supported rule by the British.

One young man, who had been drinking, told Benjamin Franklin about the declaration, "Aw, them words don't mean nothing at all." Mr. Franklin replied, "My friend, the declaration only guarantees the American people the right to pursue happiness. You have to catch it yourself!"[166]

• John F. Kennedy came from a tremendously wealthy family, and he was accused of trying to buy his Presidential election. During a campaign speech, JFK reached into his pocket and drew out what he said was a telegram from his father, the very wealthy Joseph Kennedy. JFK joked that the telegram stated, "Dear Jack, don't buy a single vote more than is necessary. I'll be d*mned if I'll pay for a landslide."[167]

• The writer of this book is a Democrat, but here's an anecdote for my Republican readers: Tom Railsback was the U.S. Representative for Illinois. Once, a newspaper boy came to his house to collect the money for his subscription to the Times *Democrat*. His young daughter Kathy opened the door, and hearing that the newspaper boy wanted money for the *Democrat*, replied, "We are all Republicans in this house," and then she shut the door.[168]

• When Len B. Jordan was running for Governor of Idaho, he was fifth of five candidates in terms of being known by the voters. Therefore, he was pleasantly surprised when he ran into a voter who said that Jordan was his second choice for Governor. When Mr. Jordan asked who his first choice was, the voter replied, "Oh, just about any one of the other four candidates."[169]

Pranks

• Minor-league umpire Scott Chestnut enjoyed playing pranks. Once, he and fellow umpire Harry "Steamboat" Johnson were staying at the old Kimball House in Atlanta, Georgia, where members of the legislature were also staying, and Mr. Chestnut decided to have some fun. He said, "Steamboat, let's talk fake foreign lingo out loud and see what these boys from down in the country think about it." Steamboat was willing, and so they jabbered at each other in a made-up language.

A crowd gathered around to hear them talk, and a member of the Georgia legislature said to Mr. Chestnut, "Mister, you sure can talk Chinese."[170]

• The One Laptop Per Child Association would like every child in a developing country to have an inexpensive laptop, some of which will be powered by a crank. Students at MIT loved the idea of power created by crank, and in 2007 the outsides of many MIT buildings began sporting cranks. (MIT students undoubtedly noticed that "crank" rhymes with "prank.") According to the MIT students, the use of cranks boosted power efficiency at MIT by 0.0005 percent.[171]

Problem-Solving

• In 2011, the city of Troy, Michigan, suffered a severe lack of money, and to reduce expenses, it considered closing its public library unless voters approved a referendum that would raise taxes .07%. A vocal anti-tax group opposed the tax increase, and it seemed as if the tax increase would be voted down and the library would be shut down. But library supporters came up with the idea of a creative campaign to convince people to vote for the tax increase and the library: "Troy Public Library would close for good unless voters approved a tax increase. With little money, six weeks until the election, facing a well-organized anti-tax group who'd managed to get two previous library-saving tax increases to fail, we had to be bold. We posed as a clandestine group who urged people to vote to close the library so they could have a book-burning party. Public outcry over the idea drowned out the anti-tax opposition and created a ground-swell of support for the library, which won by a landslide." They put these signs in yards: "VOTE TO CLOSE TROY LIBRARY AUG. 2nd. BOOK BURNING PARTY AUG. 5th. Facebook.com/BookBurningParty." The citizens of Troy, Michigan, considered the book burners to be "idiotic" and voted for the tax increase and the library. The campaign to save the library was so effective that it won an Effie Award (which recognizes effectiveness in the marketing communications industry) in the non-profit category.[172]

• In hard economic times, it helps to be creative. In 2012, Bennett Olson had a problem that needed to be solved: He lacked a job. To solve that problem, he paid $300 to advertise on an electronic billboard near downtown Minneapolis, Minnesota. For eight seconds several times during 24 hours, his photograph, his website address, and the words "Hire Me!" appeared on the billboard. The ad worked. Mr. Olson said, "After receiving quite a bit of attention, support and ultimately interviews, I felt that Laser Design & GKS Services was the right fit because they are a young, yet established company which will provide me with the opportunity to learn and grow my career." Laser Design & GKS Services is a 3D scanning company in Bloomington, Minnesota. Mr. Olson will be a sales and marketing associate there.[173]

• As kids growing up in St. Louis, Yogi Berra and his friends had little money. Fortunately, Yogi was smart and figured out a way to get footballs to play with in the streets. St. Louis University had a football team that played its games only one mile from the kids' neighborhood, and Yogi and his friends stood in the street outside the stadium. They formed a relay line with the kids standing about 30 feet apart, and whenever a football came flying over the stadium wall, Yogi would grab it and throw it to the next kid, who threw it to the next kid, until the football was safely in the kids' neighborhood and no student manager had a chance of retrieving it.[174]

• In World War II, Field Marshall Bernard Montgomery ordered the troops in England to take a five-mile run. Of course, many soldiers figured they wouldn't actually do the run. They would fall to the rear, then drop out of the run, find a quiet place to rest until the other soldiers came back, then rejoin the soldiers and run into camp. However, Field Marshall Montgomery had thought of that. He ordered everyone to be loaded into trucks, driven five miles into the country away from camp, and then dropped off. The only way to get back into camp was on your own two feet.[175]

• Rabbi Haim Jacob Widrevitz (1795-1854) once judged a dispute between a rabbi and a town. The town had fired the rabbi, but the rabbi refused to stop living in a house that was owned by the town. Rabbi Widrevitz decided that the rabbi had done nothing wrong, but since the town wished to discharge him, he would have to be discharged. However, he also judged that no one should force the rabbi to leave the house owned by the town. Instead, there was a peaceful way to resolve the situation: "All of you should move from the town and leave the rabbi alone."[176]

• How can an artist survive financially? One way is by trading art for other things. British artist Frank Bowling remembers about his friend the late American pop artist Larry Rivers, "Larry was one of the first artists who was able to trade his art for a Cadillac. He paid his doctors, his psychiatrist, everybody, by giving them art." This, Mr. Bowling says, is something to be emulated. He calls this form of commerce "marvellous. I ate in a restaurant for years without having to pay — the [owner] got three of my paintings."[177]

• Dance impresario Paul Szilard and ballerina Nora Kaye once went to see Kabuki theater in Japan. Unfortunately, Ms. Kaye grew bored during the entertainment and demanded that Mr. Szilard pull the curtains of the private box they were in. Mr. Szilard was worried that pulling the curtains might seem rude, but Ms. Kaye demanded that he do it, so he pulled them just enough that they hid Ms. Kaye, who took a nap.[178]

• As a ballerina, Allegra Kent worried about her weight. After dancing in California, she flew back to New York with several quarts of Wil Wright's ice cream (in the plane's refrigerator). The ice cream was for her family, but when they decided that they didn't want it, it ended up in Allegra's freezer, along with this note she wrote to herself: "Allegra Kent, Keep Out."[179]

• Catharine Shipley, a Quaker, was out walking when someone tried to grab her purse. She held on tight to her purse, and told the would-be thief, "We'll kneel right down here and ask Heavenly Father if He means thee to have it." Apparently, the would-be thief wasn't in a praying mood because he ran away.[180]

• Nathan Strauss went to Lakewood, New Jersey, and attempted to register at Hotel Eureka. However, a clerk noted that Mr. Strauss was a Jew and told him that the hotel had no room for him. Shortly afterward, Mr. Strauss returned to the hotel and fired the clerk — Mr. Strauss had bought the hotel.[181]

Public Speaking

• Rabbi Stephen Wise (1874-1949) once spoke at a rally against Nazis. In the days before the rally, he received anonymous threats saying that he would be shot if he spoke at the anti-Nazi rally. When it was his turn to speak, he stood up and began by saying, "If anyone is going to shoot me, let him do it now. I hate to be interrupted." By the way, Rabbi Wise frequently denounced unethical politicians from the pulpit. Once he was introduced to a politician who said, "You don't need to introduce me. I know who he is; after all, he's denounced me often enough from the pulpit." Rabbi Wise replied, "You are wrong, sir. I've denounced you often, but not often enough."[182]

• Winston Churchill found innovative ways of distracting other people's attention from speeches he disagreed with. Once, while Hugh Todd Naylor Gaitskell was giving a speech on economic affairs, Mr. Churchill suddenly sat straight up, looked around him, went through all his pockets, then started searching the floor, all the time pretending not to notice that everyone's attention was on him, not on Mr. Gaitskell. Finally, Mr. Churchill explained, "I was only looking for my jujube." (A jujube is a piece of candy.)[183]

• Winston Churchill made many speeches. Before addressing an audience in the United States, a woman asked him how it felt to have his speeches so well attended. Sir Winston replied, "It's quite flattering, but whenever I feel this way I always remember that if instead of making a political speech I was being hanged, the crowd would be twice as big."[184]

• While running for President, Adlai Stevenson campaigned extensively in Florida. While campaigning in California, he was asked if he played golf by a woman who had noticed his deep tan. Mr. Stevenson explained that he had gotten the tan making outdoor speeches in Florida. The woman replied, "If you got that brown making speeches, you talked too long."[185]

Religion

• Here are a few anecdotes about religion: 1) A young boy lying in a hospital bed moved and unknowingly pressed the call button for the nurses' station. A male nurse answered the call and asked through the intercom, "Yes, Bobby?" The young boy was startled and remained silent. The male nurse asked, "Bobby, are you there?" Bobby answered, "Yes, God." 2) A young child was asked if her family had a real Christmas tree or an artificial Christmas tree. She replied, "We have a real one, like the Bible says." 3) An elderly churchgoer had arthritis, so her doctor told her not to get on her knees unless the Lord was coming. 4) The signboard outside a church once proclaimed two messages: the top message said, "Pastor Bob is on vacation," and the bottom message said, "Praise the Lord!" 5) A church once posted this message on its signboard out front: "We're going to heaven someday. If you need a ride, give us a call." 6) A church newsletter once stated, "Council Report — Due to the length of the Parish Council meeting, very little business was conducted."[186]

• Here are some jokes and anecdotes on religious subjects: 1) A new church secretary had previously worked for the Pentagon — he labeled the church files as "Sacred" and "Top Sacred." 2) A man was heckling a Salvation Army worker: "Do you believe that Jonah spent three days in the belly of a whale?" "I don't know," she answered. "I'll ask him when I get to Heaven." "But what if he isn't there?" asked the heckler. The Salvation Army worker replied, "Then you ask him." 3) A farmer sadly surveyed his acreage, all of which was a foot under water because of a flood. "The Lord may be good, and the Lord may be just," the farmer said, "but He doesn't know a thing about farming." 4) Sign outside a church: "Sin now. Pay later." 5) A little girl prayed to God, "Please watch after Daddy." After a moment's thought, she added, "And You'd better keep an eye on Mommy, too."[187]

• A man claiming to be a prophet of God was brought before a skeptical Caliph, who said, "All prophets have been given a gift by God. If you are a prophet, you will be able to prove it by showing us your gift." The man claiming to a prophet replied, "You are right — all prophets have been given a gift by God. My gift is the ability to read men's minds. Allow me to demonstrate: Right now you are thinking that I am not a prophet." In another case, a man who claimed to be God was brought before a skeptical Caliph, who said, "Recently, a man claimed to be a prophet sent from God. I had him put in a mental institution." "You did the right thing," replied the man who claimed to be God. "I didn't send him."[188]

• A merchant had an ethical dilemma, so he came to R' Chaim Elazar, the Rav of Kalish, for advice. The merchant wished to conclude a business deal that would be highly profitable for him, but which required that he engage in a small act of deception. Would the deception be permitted? R' Chaim Elazar replied, "You know that the Ten Commandments were written on both sides of the tablets (*Shemos* 32:15). That teaches you that no matter how you turn them, they still read, 'Thou shalt not steal.'"[189]

• A maggid was noted for his sermons in which he castigated people for their sins. The sermons were very moving, and they caused many people to repent. After the maggid died, the sermons were published, but although the words were the same, they had lost their power to move people. What was missing was the maggid's deep sighs as he spoke about sin.[190]

• Isaac Hopper was a Quaker and a fervent abolitionist. In fact, he was too fervent of an abolitionist for some of the Quakers he worshipped with, so they dropped him from the records of the meeting. Nevertheless, Mr. Hopper continued to attend meeting. When he was told that the meeting had disowned him, he replied, "But I have not disowned the meeting."[191]

• At Fort Custer, Michigan, a soldier who was a Protestant needed to see a chaplain, but the only available chaplain was a Catholic. The Protestant soldier said that he was afraid that the Catholic chaplain would try to change his faith, but the Catholic chaplain replied, "My son, I don't want you to change your faith. I want your faith to change you."[192]

• According to the Hasidic masters, to love God you must first love human beings. If anyone ever tells you that he loves God but he does not love his fellow human beings, he is lying.[193]

Revenge

• Hugh Troy once was annoyed by very nosy, very stuffy neighbors after he moved to Washington, D.C. To get even, he ordered very large metal numbers from a hardware store, and paid the delivery person to knock on his neighbors' doors and ask if this was the house that wanted the large numbers on the doors. Next, he ordered weekly deliveries of large numbers of sheets and towels — and made sure the neighbors heard about it. Finally, he invited the many secretaries at work to visit his new house in a group. The neighbors were shocked and afraid that Mr. Troy was going to open a bawdy house on their very respectable street. They even formed a committee and hired a lawyer to stop Mr. Troy before finding out that they were the victims of a put-on.[194]

• As a young man, Bud Abbott of Abbott and Costello fame was shanghaied and forced to work aboard a Norwegian ship. In addition to shoveling coal, he taught the English language to the Norwegian sailors. As revenge, he taught them that the proper way to say "Thank you" in English was to say "F— you." By the way, Mr. Abbott was an epileptic. Whenever Lou Costello noticed that Mr. Abbott was about to have a seizure, he stopped it from occurring by punching him hard in the stomach.[195]

• African-American comedian Angela Scott talks about an apartment becoming vacant in her building. She wanted to have a friend move into it, but the landlord wouldn't allow that. Therefore, whenever the landlord showed the apartment to white people, she wore curlers in her hair, put on slippers and a housecoat, went out on her landing, and loudly said, "Le*roy*, don't start no sh*t. You put that knife down. Come out here, kids, all twenty of you."[196]

• Nicholas Longworth, an Ohio politician who was the Speaker of the House of Representatives in the 1920s, got annoyed whenever anyone made fun of his baldness. Once, a politician with a full head of hair felt Mr. Longworth's bald head, then said, "Feels just like my wife's bottom." Mr. Longworth got his revenge on the politician by also feeling his bald head, then remarking, "Yes, it does."[197]

• Producer Irving Thalberg once kept the Marx Brothers waiting, although they had an appointment, so the Marx Brothers took comic revenge. They lit cigars and blew smoke under the door of Mr. Thalberg's office until he was forced to let them in.[198]

Chapter 5: From Sports to Zen

Sports

• Here are some miscellaneous ice-skating facts: 1) Figure skater Elvis Stojko is named after Elvis Presley. Although it seemed natural for him to skate to Elvis' music, he resisted doing so for years, waiting until exactly the right moment. In January 1994, after he won his first Canadian national championship, he skated to Elvis' music at the exhibition. Only three people knew about the program beforehand — it was a surprise even to his Elvis Presley-loving parents. 2) Figure skater Scott Hamilton is only five foot, three inches tall — the result of Schwachmann's syndrome, a rare disease that inhibits growth in children. Mr. Hamilton's short stature didn't hurt his skating career at all — he won four consecutive world championships and an Olympic gold medal and has a flourishing professional career. 3) In 1911, Ludowika Eilers of Germany and Walter Jacobsson of Finland won the world pairs skating championship — they were the only pairs team to show up. 4) As a young boy, John Curry was mesmerized by the Royal Ballet in England. He asked to take ballet lessons — his parents wouldn't let him, but they did let him take skating lessons after he saw an ice show on television. As an adult, Mr. Curry brought a balletic grace to figure skating and he made artistry an important part of skating. 5) Canadian pairs skaters Michelle Menzies and Jean-Michel Bombardier used to wear a symbol consisting of an arrow pointing straight up — which was where they wanted their career in figure skating to go.[199]

• Here are a few miscellaneous sports anecdotes: 1) Gymnast Mary Lou Retton was once asked whether training for the Olympics and missing school had hurt her education. She replied, "While other kids were reading about the Great Wall, I was walking on it." 2) Janet Lynn is a famous ice skater in part because of a mistake she made in the 1972 Olympic Games in Japan. She fell during a spin, ruining her chance for a gold medal, but smiled. That smile under duress made her admired worldwide and especially by the Japanese. 3) Christopher Bowman was a figure skater whose bad habits kept him from being the success he might have been. People who knew him called him "Hans Brinker from Hell."[200]

• Here are a few miscellaneous gymnastics anecdotes: 1) Olympic gymnast Mitch Gaylord worked as the stunt double for Robin in the movie *Batman Forever*. However, an explosion misfired on the Batboat and almost killed him. Now, he sticks to safe acting roles. 2) Gymnasts have to be tough. In a competition, a ripped callus on Jair Lynch's hand was bothering him, so he used a razor blade to cut it off, then he performed on the parallel bars with bloody hands. 3) Peter Vidmar began taking gymnastics lessons with Makodo Sakamodo after he saw the renowned coach's ad in a newspaper: "Future Olympic Champions Sought." Mr. Vidmar won gold and silver at the 1984 Olympics.[201]

• Kelly McCormick won her Olympic medals in springboard diving, but she started out as a gymnast. She did become an elite gymnast, but she used to go on vacation to ski and whenever she returned from vacation, she would be dropped a class. Finally, she grew angry enough to quit gymnastics and take up diving. When Kelly's mother, Pat McCormick (who won four Olympic gold medals as a diver) was a girl, she entered a pier-to-pier competition in which she swam from one pier to another pier placed two or three miles out into the ocean. She came in second — but there were only two swimmers in the competition.[202]

• In the old days of figure skating, competitions were held outside, causing hardship for both the skaters and the judges. Canadian judge John Machado once spent six hours in a blizzard, judging men's figures during the 1936 Olympics in Germany. He finally was forced to leave the ice because he contracted pneumonia. By the way, the Canadians are serious about ice skating. They sometimes simulate competitions

— complete with judges, camera flashes, and television cameras — to ready their skaters for the real thing.[203]

• As a young skater, Robert Davenport had great strength but little control. When he performed jumps, the audience would gasp because it looked as if he would come crashing down on the ice (indeed, he sometimes did). Members of the audience used to say, "He's a kamikaze." By the way, even young athletes can feel stress. When Peggy Fleming was a young figure skater, she was too nervous to keep food in her stomach before an important competition, so her mother used to give her protein drinks.[204]

• When Tiger Woods began to play as a freshman on the Stanford University golf team, his teammates treated him like any other freshman, although he had already won several important amateur golf tournaments. They teased him, they made him carry the extra luggage, and they made him sit in the front of the bus — next to the coach. By the way, Tiger became a multi-millionaire as soon as he turned pro, signing contracts worth $60 million with Nike and Titleist on August 28, 1996.[205]

• Olympic medal-winning swimmer Jenny Thompson was incredibly focused on winning. In 1994, she broke her arm, and shortly afterward, her coach discovered her working out in the gym despite her stitches — something that was definitely against her doctor's orders.[206]

• Russian Svetlana Khorkina is 5-foot-5 and 105 pounds, making her a giant among elite women's gymnasts. Want to know how to recognize her at a gymnastics meet? It's not difficult. She says, "I'm very easy to see on the podium, because everyone else is *small.*"[207]

• International students make major contributions to the colleges and universities where they study. In 1981, the University of Texas — El Paso won the NCAA Track and Field Championships. Not one of its 70 points was scored by a USAmerican.[208]

Succoth

• Rabbi Shlomo Carlebach took shopping for an essrog to celebrate Succoth (the Jewish Feast of Tabernacles) seriously. For hours, he would look at all the essrog tables, scrutinizing each essrog carefully, touching it, and even smelling it. Because he was looking for a perfect essrog, he rejected many, many essrogs. But each time he rejected an essrog, he would kiss it and murmur a few words of apology before continuing his search for a perfect essrog.[209]

Television

• During the question-and-answer session at the beginning of her TV variety show, Carol Burnett was asked what her measurements were. She replied, "37-24-38 — but not necessarily in that order." Early in her career, Ms. Burnett mugged a lot. During the beginning of one of her television shows, a member of the audience asked if her mouth was insured. She joked, "There isn't enough money!" Ms. Burnett seems so down to earth that it is difficult to think of her as the big Hollywood star she is. She sometimes receives letters that say such things as, "Dear Carol, I know this sounds crazy, but I really admire you."[210]

• Ed Sullivan occasionally made mistakes when talking about his guests. On the Sunday before his first appearance on Mr. Sullivan's TV show, Terry-Thomas watched the show and heard Mr. Sullivan mention him in this way: "Don't forget to watch next week, folks. We've got a wonderful show for you. We have England's top television star, Tommy Tucker."[211]

Tobacco

• Quakers tend to be against smoking. Once, Sojourner Truth smoked a corncob pipe at the house of some Quakers she was staying with. One of her hosts asked, "Sojourner, when thee gets to Heaven, what will God say when he smells thy breath strong of tobacco?" Ms. Truth replied, "When I get to Heaven, I expect to leave my breath behind." By the way, Amos Kenworthy, a Quaker, passed by a group of men, one of whom was smoking. The smoker asked him, "Won't you join us?" Mr. Kenworthy replied, "I don't like thy smell."[212]

• Before George Burns and Gracie Allen were married, Mr. Burns had a rival. Once, Ms. Allen was ill and in a hospital, and Mr. Burns was supposed to tell her beau the news. Mr. Burns didn't do that, so the beau didn't send flowers — but Mr. Burns filled her hospital room with baskets of flowers. By the way, Mr. Burns smoked cigars on stage, but he was always careful not to blow smoke into his wife's face. He always walked out on stage to find out which way the smoke would blow before his and Gracie's act.[213]

Umpires

• Bill Kinnamon's first game as a major-league umpire saw him at third base with very little to do — no close calls at all. One player hit a ball that was foul by about 30 feet down the third-base line. Mr. Kinnamon says, "I ran over and waved my arm, signaling 'foul ball' as if it was a big deal, just to have something to do." By the way, Mr. Kinnamon was working on October 1, 1961, when Roger Maris hit his 61st home run of the season to break Babe Ruth's old record. Mr. Kinnamon says that he made a mistake after the game — as was his habit, he ripped up the lineup card and threw it away. If he had kept it, it would be worth a small fortune. When Mr. Maris hit his 61st home run of the season on October 1, 1961, the new record was controversial because Mr. Maris' season was longer than Mr. Ruth's season, and so Mr. Maris had more games in which to set the new record. Boston Red Sox player Pete Runnels was at first base. He turned to umpire John "Red" Flaherty and said, "I don't care what anybody says — it tingles the spine." Red says, "I had to agree."[214]

• Around the beginning of the century, Wild Bill Donovan was pitching for Detroit when he saw his catcher signal for a pitchout. (A pitchout is a pitch deliberately thrown outside of the strike zone in an attempt to catch a base runner stealing.) Wild Bill was shocked at the signal, because there were no runners on base. However, his catcher came out to talk to him and explained the situation, which was this. Tim Hurst was umpiring the game, and Umpire Hurst had been insulted all day by the batter. Since Umpire Hurst did not take kindly to insults, he had told the batter that no matter what the next pitch was, he was going to call it a strike. Wild Bill agreed to throw a pitchout, and he threw a pitch that was three feet outside of the strike zone. Umpire Hurst called a strike — as he had promised — and the batter registered a strong protest, only to be thrown out of the game.[215]

• Long ago, a man named Morgan umpired in the Western League. In one game, he made a series of calls against the home team, which mightily upset their fans. After yet another call against the home team, a homegrown fan let loose with a torrent of particularly abusive epithets against the umpire. This made umpire Morgan mad, so he called a time out, then faced the stands and shouted, "The man who shouted those things is a coward. He doesn't have the courage to stand up and admit that he shouted those things. If he does have the courage — which I doubt — let him stand up now." After hearing this, every man in the stands stood up.[216]

• After a balk was called on a Dodger pitcher, the Dodgers left their positions and started squawking. Umpire Jocko Conlan wasn't about to stand for that, so he put a couple of fingers in his watch pocket and said, "You've got two minutes to clear the field. Two minutes or I'll forfeit this ball game. If you don't think I will, stay here." The Dodgers returned to their positions, except for first baseman Dolf Camilli, who was a nice guy. He asked Mr. Conlan, "What time is it?" Mr. Conlan growled, "None of your business," and Mr. Camilli grinned, then said, "I thought so." He had guessed — correctly — that Mr. Conlan didn't have a watch.[217]

• The first black major-league umpire was Emmett Ashford. He and white umpire Tom Gorman once worked a game at spring training in which Brooks Robinson took a feeble swing at the ball, but protested when Mr. Gorman called a strike, saying that he really didn't swing at the ball. Mr. Robinson asked Mr. Gorman to see what his umpiring partner thought, and Mr. Ashford said, "Yeah, man, he swung at the ball." Mr. Gorman then said to Mr. Robinson, "Okay, Brooks, now you've got it in black and white."[218]

• Umpire Eric Gregg disliked Larry Bowa, who got on umpires a lot, both as a player and as a manager. Once, Mr. Bowa was batting when Mr. Gregg was umpiring at first base. He hit the ball, ran hard for first, and managed to knock Mr. Gregg over. Mr. Gregg lay in the dirt, groggy and in pain, and he heard over him someone asking, "Safe or out? Safe or out?" He said, "Who's asking?" The answer came, "Bowa," and Mr. Gregg said, "Bowa's out."[219]

Underground Jokes

• Food and clothing were often scarce under Soviet rule, even in the state stores, as shown in these underground jokes: 1) A Russian traveler asked a Lithuanian farmer at a market what price he wanted for his apples. The farmer replied that he wanted three rubles a pound. The customer protested, "At the state store, apples are only one ruble a pound." The farmer said, "Then go buy your apples at the state store." "I can't," the customer said, " because the state store is out of apples." The farmer shrugged, then said, "If I were out of apples, I would also sell them for only one ruble a pound." 2) Goods such as clothing were scarce under Soviet rule. One of the many statues of Vladimir Lenin depicted him with one hand holding on to his coat lapel while another hand pointed forward, in the general direction of Finland. Lithuanians sometimes secretly placed this sign on the statue: "Where did I get this coat? There, in Finland."[220]

• Aleksandr Solzhenitsyn's novels such as *Cancer Ward* were unavailable in the Soviet Union, but they were smuggled out of the country, translated, and published abroad. This led to an underground joke: Q: Do Soviets read the novels of Solzhenitsyn? A: Yes, but only if they can read a language other than Russian.[221]

War

• Colin Powell was accepted by both New York University and the City College of New York in 1954. Deciding which college to attend was easy — yearly tuition at NYU was $750, while yearly tuition at CCNY was only $10. By the way, while in Korea, Mr. Powell became the victim of a *punji* trap set by a North Vietnamese soldier. A simple *punji* trap was a sharpened stick placed in a camouflaged hole; the tip of the stick was often coated with animal dung to create an infection in any wound caused by the stick. Mr. Powell's wound was not serious, but he was forced to go to Saigon for treatment. Also by the way, while serving in the Vietnam War, Mr. Powell was shocked when he learned that South Vietnamese soldiers were using machine gun fire to cut down trees. He spoke to Captain Vo Cong Hieu, the leader of the South Vietnamese troops, and told him how much each machine gun bullet cost. Captain Hieu quickly figured out on his own how wasteful cutting down trees with machine gun fire was, and he quickly stopped the practice.[222]

• General George McClellan was not overeager to fight during the Civil War. Instead, he kept pestering President Abraham Lincoln for more men. An exasperated President Lincoln bore it for a while, then said, "If I gave McClellan all the men he asks for, they couldn't find room to lie down. They would all have to sleep standing up." Once, President Lincoln complained of General McClellan's inactivity, then said, "If McClellan doesn't want to use the army for a while, I'd like to borrow it from him for a while and see if I can't do something or other with it." Eventually, President Lincoln fired General McClellan for non-aggressiveness.[223]

• When Hugh Troy was inducted into the Air Corps, he was asked if he had any special skills so they could be punched into a MOS (Military Operation Specialty) card that would label him with those skills forever. The card would determine his military training and military job. The man asking him questions was interrupted and had to leave to answer a telephone call, so Mr. Troy used the time to punch eight holes at random in his MOS card. As a result of those random punches, Mr. Troy was classified as a demolition expert! During World

War II, he performed his job well, teaching soldiers how to find and defuse booby traps.[224]

Wit and Wisdom

• Noël Coward had a sharp and ready wit: 1) He listened as Mantovani and his orchestra rehearsed a song that he had written. Suddenly, Mr. Coward pointed to a musician and said, "That violinist has an unerring instinct for putting his finger on the wrong note." 2) Mr. Coward once saw a play starring a 14-year-old actor. Afterward, he said, "Two things should have been cut. The second act and that youngster's throat." 3) Mr. Coward was late for his airplane when a reporter blocked his way and asked, "Mr. Coward. Haven't you anything to say to *The Star*?" Mr. Coward replied, "Yes — twinkle." 4) Mr. Coward was known as "The Master." When asked about the nickname, Mr. Coward replied, "Jack of all trades, master of none." 5) Mr. Coward remained slim throughout his life. When asked how he managed this, Mr. Coward replied, "An iron will, dear boy — and not enough calories." 6) Mr. Coward once heard that a man he did not respect had committed suicide by blowing his brains out. He commented, "He must have been an incredibly good shot." 7) To his friends the Redgraves, Mr. Coward sent a gift. It was a framed photograph in a silver frame — the photograph showed Noël Coward looking at a bust of Noël Coward, and it was signed, "Noël Coward."[225]

• Bahlul, the wise fool, was met by a Caliph, who asked him where he was coming from. "I am returning from Hell," Bahlul explained. "My fire was out, so I went to Hell to get more fire, but the chief Devil said that there was no fire in Hell — there's no need to have any fire there, for everyone who goes to Hell brings his own fire with him." By the way, Bahlul once sat on a Caliph's throne in the Caliph's absence. Immediately, the Caliph's guards grabbed Bahlul and beat him. Bahlul began crying, and when the Caliph walked into the room, he asked Bahlul why he was crying. Bahlul explained, "I am not crying for my sake, but for yours. If I am beaten this way for sitting on your throne for a moment, what beatings must be in store for you, who have sat on the throne for years!"[226]

• In 1952, Adlai Stevenson ran against Dwight D. Eisenhower for President of the United States. The working press respected Mr. Stevenson. In Kansas City, Mr. Stevenson tripped and would have fallen on his face if a couple of photographers had not dropped their cameras so they could catch him. Chances are, the photographers would not have done this for another politician, as one photographer was heard to say, "If that'd only been Eisenhower, we would have had a Pulitzer." By the way, when Mr. Stevenson heard that a platform that General Eisenhower was standing on had collapsed, he commented, "I'm glad the General wasn't hurt. But I wasn't surprised that it happened — I've been telling him for two months that nobody could stand on that platform."[227]

• Comedian Jack Benny used many gestures in his comedy, including a hand-to-cheek gesture. According to Mr. Benny's friend, George Burns, Mr. Benny developed this gesture in order to have something to do with his hands. In vaudeville, Mr. Benny had carried a violin. On the radio, he had held the script. On television, he wasn't quite sure what to do with his hands — thus he developed the hand-to-cheek gesture. By the way, Oscar Levant once asked Mr. Benny's friend Fred Allen, "Fred, are you an egomaniac?" Mr. Allen replied, "No, Oscar. I've heard that the meek shall inherit the earth and I'm standing by to collect."[228]

• Abraham Lincoln was a plain-spoken man. In Springfield, Illinois, Mr. Lincoln's law partner, William Herndon, spoke volumes of eloquence about the beauty and wonder of Niagara Falls, then he asked Mr. Lincoln what had most impressed him about seeing the waterfalls. Mr. Lincoln replied, "The thing that struck me most forcibly when I saw the Falls was, where in the world did all that water come from?" By the way, name-calling in politics is not new. In a debate, Stephen

Douglas called Abraham Lincoln "two-faced." Mr. Lincoln asked Mr. Douglas, "I leave it to you. If I had another face, would I wear this one?"[229]

• According to the Jews, days begin at sunset. All Sabbaths and festivals and holidays also begin at sunset. Why? It is easy to have faith when the sun is shining. Days begin at sunset to symbolize the faith, present in the darkness, that another dawn will occur. By the way, two rabbis debated when night ends. One rabbi said, "Night ends when you can tell the difference between a blue thread and a purple thread. Another rabbi said, "Night ends when you can see the face of your brother."[230]

• Dorothy Parker loved playing word games. During a word-game session at the Algonquin Hotel, she was challenged to use the word "horticulture" in a sentence. She said, "You can lead a wh*re to culture, but you can't make her think." By the way, at a party, someone asked Ms. Parker, "Are you Dorothy Parker?" She replied, "Yes. Do you mind?" Also by the way, after getting an abortion, Ms. Parker said, "It serves me right for putting all my eggs in one bast*rd."[231]

• Nicholas Waln (1742-1813) was both a Quaker and a wit. A lawyer, he adopted the Quakers' plain style of dress after he converted. Some of his fellow lawyers thought this was funny, and they decided to make fun of his long-brimmed hat. One lawyer said to him mockingly, "There is a great deal of dignity and intelligence under that hat of yours." Mr. Waln immediately took off his hat, and handed it to the mocker, saying, "Take it. Thou hast need of both."[232]

• Thomas Whittemore, a Representative in the Massachusetts legislature, once spoke out against legislators voting on a bill to increase their own wages. Nevertheless, the wage increase was voted in with a large majority. Afterward, Representative Whittemore was asked about the vote. He replied, "Naturally I am disappointed by the action taken on the bill; but I guess I can do nothing now but pocket the insult."[233]

• George Washington once visited a little person (formerly known as a midget or a dwarf). The little person was severely handicapped and unable to sit up on his own; however, he had a remarkable wit. When Mr. Washington asked him if he had been a Whig or a Tory in the Revolutionary War, the little person replied, "I have never taken an *active* part on either side."[234]

• Rabbi Yitzchak Feigenbaum of Warsaw once was asked to judge a dispute between a father and a son. While the father and the son presented their arguments to the Rabbi, the son kept mocking his father. Finally, Rabbi Feigenbaum said that he could not fairly judge their dispute, because the son's mocking of his father had prejudiced him by causing him to hate the son.[235]

• Morris K. Udall helped clean up the loose ends in the Pacific after the Allies won World War II. While helping to close the base on Iwo Jima, Mr. Udall served as emcee of a variety show. At the end of the show, Mr. Udall said, "Gentlemen, I guarantee you this next act will bring down the house," and a bulldozer demolished the wooden stage.[236]

• While on a trip, the Chofetz Chayim went to sleep, only to awake to find his fellow passengers engaged in argument. When he asked the subject of the controversy, a passenger said, "We are discussing horses." The Chofetz Chayim replied, "An excellent subject. It's much better to talk about horses than to gossip about human beings."[237]

• The Hasidic master Israel of Rizhin was once asked how to repent. Israel asked, "Did you know how to sin?" The sinner replied, "That was easy. First I sinned, then I knew what sin is." So Israel told the sinner, "First repent, then you will know what repentance is."[238]

Work

• Merrill Ashley worked very hard to become a member, then a soloist, and then a principal of the New York City Ballet. After Ms. Ashley had danced exceedingly well in the premiere of Jacques d'Amboise's *Saltarelli*, someone asked George Balanchine, "Wasn't she beautiful, Mr. B?" Mr. Balanchine agreed, "Oh, yes! In three or four years, very good dancer." This was praise, but not exactly the kind of praise Ms. Ashley was hoping for. For one thing, she was hoping for a raise and a promotion soon. She thought, "I'll show him." Sure enough, it was not too long before she was given a raise and a promotion to soloist. (Even before those things happened, Mr. Balanchine had given her a rare compliment after she first danced in *Diamonds*: "Excellent, dear.") One season, Ms. Ashley thought that she would be made a principal dancer, but she was disappointed. She explained to Peter Martins her disappointment and asked him if she should speak to master choreographer George Balanchine, the man who decided who got promotions, but Mr. Martins advised her about her disappointment, "Swallow it. Just swallow it." Fortunately, she was promoted to principal dancer not too long afterward.[239]

• W.C. Fields was a juggler before he was a comedian, and he showed much determination in learning how to juggle. "I still carry scars on my legs from those early attempts at juggling," he stated. "I'd balance a stick on my toe, toss it in the air, and try to catch it again on my toe. Hour after hour the d*mn thing would bang against my shinbones. I'd work until tears were streaming down my face. But I kept on practicing, and bleeding, until I perfected the trick. I don't believe that Mozart, Liszt, Paderewski, or Kreisler ever worked any harder than I did." Mr. Fields seems to have learned some of his comedic technique from his mother. Mrs. Dukinfield (Mr. Fields was born William Claude Dukinfield) would stand in her doorway, talk to passersby, and criticize them under her breath so only her son could hear her.[240]

• A member of President Abraham Lincoln's cabinet was ambitious to be President, and some of President Lincoln's friends advised him to squelch the cabinet-member's ambition. However, President Lincoln said the situation reminded him of a time when he was plowing with a slow horse, and suddenly the horse began pushing the plow so quickly that he had to run to keep up with the horse and the plow. When he came to the end of the row, he looked at the horse and discovered that a chin-fly was biting the horse, so he knocked it off. His brother had then criticized him, saying that the chin-fly was the only thing making the horse go. President Lincoln then told his advisors about the cabinet-member, "If he has a Presidential chin-fly biting him, I'm not going to knock it off, if it will only make his department go."[241]

• Some jobs lead to unusual experiences. Mary Bacon worked as a jockey in the 1970s, when few racing facilities had dressing rooms specifically set up for women. Often, she found herself dressing in the first-aid room. At a Florida racetrack, an elderly man suffered a heart attack and died, and his corpse was put in the first-aid room. Ms. Bacon said, "I'm not changing in front of a dead man." By the way, while doing her job, her face used to be caked by the mud flying out from under the hooves of the racing horses. She once told the *New York Daily News*, "Some women shell out $25 for a mud pack and I get 'em for free."[242]

• Be careful whose contract you don't renew. In 1986, the figure-skating touring show Ice Capades decided not to renew Scott Hamilton's contract. Big mistake. Mr. Hamilton, a four-time men's World Champion and an Olympic gold medalist, created his own show and named it Stars on Ice. Today, it is a major show, traveling to over 70 North American cities and appearing as a special on TV. By the way, Canadian figure skater Kurt Browning performed a version of Gene Kelly's classic dance "Singing in the Rain" in his 1994 TV special, *You Must Remember This*. The four-minute program took 10 hours to film.[243]

• Paul Laurence Dunbar, who was born in Dayton, Ohio, was the first African American to make his living as a writer. His father, Joshua, had been a slave who escaped to Canada on the Underground Railroad, passing through Cincinnati and Dayton. During the Civil War, he left Canada to fight on the side of the North. Mr. Dunbar was a hard worker. Will Marion Cook and he once wrote a hit musical titled *Clorindy, the Origin of the Cakewalk*, in one night. They sat down at a kitchen table one evening and wrote all the songs, all the lyrics, and all the dialogue by 4 a.m.[244]

• Penny Ann Early was one of the first women jockeys in the United States. As such, she was faced with tremendous amounts of prejudice. Because of the difficulty in finding horses to ride, she stopped racing for a while to play professional women's basketball, and she described her qualifications for doing so in this way: "I played in high school. It was in gym class." By the way, after woman jockey Joan O'Shea lost a race, a man in the crowd yelled to her, "Go home where you belong and cook dinner!" She replied, "I can't cook, either."[245]

• The TV series *Roseanne* was about the working-class. In one episode, Roseanne asked her husband how his day at work went. He replied, "Well, today was a special one for me. It was the 179th day in a row where I did exactly the same thing." In another episode, Roseanne went to a trailer park to visit her daughter. Another woman (played by Sharon Stone) in the trailer park thought Roseanne lived there, but Roseanne said, "Whaddaya think, we're made of money? We rent!"[246]

• The Rev. Jerry Robbins was a new and young pastor, and he was worried about how he would be received by the people in his church. He decided to visit a new member, so he rang the doorbell, and noticing a newspaper on the welcome mat, he picked it up so he could give it to the new member. A girl answered the door, looked at him, and then yelled for her mother: "Mom, it's the newspaper boy."[247]

• Pope John XXIII came from peasant origins. He once explained, "In Italy, there are three ways of losing one's money — women, gambling, and farming. My father chose the most boring of the three." By the way, when Pope John XXIII met a group of refrigerator salesmen, he said, "You are welcome though our jobs are distinct and far apart. Ours is to warm hearts."[248]

Zen

• Here are some Zen anecdotes: 1) When some Western Zen students asked Zen master Taisen Deshimaru what people should do in their everyday lives, he replied, "Work, go to the toilet, eat; whatever you like." 2) Zen master Muso Kokushi (1275-1351) had high praise for his student, the shogun Takauji, saying that Takauji put in long hours of meditation even after a night of heavy drinking. 3) Zen master Soen Roshi sometimes played tricks on his Western Zen students. He would invite students to a sutra-chanting contest, then at its conclusion tell them there was no one winner because "Everyone is best!" 4) Zen master Soen Roshi was eccentric. He took the Zen motto of Bodhidharma — "Nothing holy" — seriously, so he sometimes conducted the tea ceremony using soda or coffee instead of tea. 5) A famous Zen poem by P'ang Yun ends with the lines, "My supernatural power and marvelous activity: / Drawing water and chopping wood."[249]

• Here are two Zen stories: 1) At the end of his life, Zen master Ikkyu told his disciples, "After my death some of you will seclude yourselves in the forests and mountains to meditate, while others may drink sake and enjoy the company of women. Both kinds of Zen are fine, but if some become professional clerics, babbling about 'Zen as the Way,' they are my enemies." 2) Zen Master Takuan Soho was dying, so his disciples asked him for his last words. At first, Takuan Soho said that he had no last words, but his disciples really wanted a last message from him, so he picked up a paintbrush, wrote the character for "dream," and then died.[250]

Appendix A: Bibliography

Aaseng, Nate. *Great Winter Olympic Moments*. Minneapolis, MN: Lerner Publications Company, 1990.

Adams, Joey. *The God Bit*. Boston, MA: G.K. Hall & Co., 1975.

Allen, Steve. *More Funny People*. New York: Stein and Day, Publishers, 1982.

Alley, Ken. *Awkward Christian Soldiers*. Wheaton, IL: Harold Shaw Publishers, 1998.

Ashley, Merrill. *Dancing for Balanchine*. New York: E.P. Dutton, Inc., 1984.

Backus, Jim and Henny. *Forgive Us Our Digressions*. New York: St. Martin's Press, 1988.

Berra, Yogi. *"I Really Didn't Say Everything I Said."* New York: Workman Publishing Company, Inc., 1998.

Besserman, Perle and Manfred Steger. *Crazy Clouds: Zen Radicals, Rebels, and Reformers*. Boston, MA: Shambhala, 1991.

Bezic, Sandra. *The Passion to Skate: An Intimate View of Figure Skating*. With David Hayes. Atlanta, GA: Turner Publishing, Inc., 1996.

Blackman, Sushila, compiler and editor. *Graceful Exits: How Great Beings Die*. New York: Weatherhill, Inc., 1997.

Brandreth, Gyles. *Great Theatrical Disasters*. New York: St. Martin's Press, 1982.

Brennan, Christine. *Inside Edge: A Revealing Journey into the Secret World of Figure Skating*. New York: Scribner, 1996.

Charles, Helen White, collector and editor. *Quaker Chuckles and Other True Stories About Friends*. Oxford, OH: H.W. Charles, 1961.

Clercq, Tanaquil Le. *The Ballet Cook Book*. New York: Stein and Day, Publishers, 1966.

Collins, Beulah, collector. *For Benefit of Clergy*. New York: Grosset & Dunlap, 1966.

Conlan, Jocko and Robert W. Creamer. *Jocko*. Lincoln, NE: University of Nebraska Press, 1997.

Crow, Bill. *Jazz Anecdotes*. New York: Oxford University Press, 1990.

Deedy, John. *A Book of Catholic Anecdotes*. Allen, TX: Thomas More, 1997.

Dickinson, Joy Wallace. *Remembering Orlando: Tales from Elvis to Disney*. Charleston, South Carolina: The History Press, 2006.

Dole, Bob. *Great Political Wit*. New York: Doubleday, 1998.

Dole, Bob. *Great Presidential Wit*. New York: Scribner, 2001.

Eichenbaum, Rose. *Masters of Movement: Portraits of America's Great Choreographers*. Washington DC: Smithsonian Books, 2004.

Epstein, Lawrence J. *A Treasury of Jewish Anecdotes*. Northvale, NJ: Jason Aronson, Inc., 1989.

Fadiman, James and Robert Frager. *Essential Sufism*. San Francisco, CA: HarperSanFrancisco, 1997.

Farzan, Massud. *Another Way of Laughter: A Collection of Sufi Humor*. New York: E.P. Dutton & Co., Inc., 1973.

Finlayson, Reggie. *Colin Powell*. Minneapolis, MN: Lerner Publications Company, 1997.

Foster, Leila Merrell. *Benjamin Franklin: Founding Father and Inventor*. Springfield, NJ: Enslow Publications, Inc., 1997.

Garagiola, Joe. *Baseball is a Funny Game*. New York: Bantam Books, 1960.

Garagiola, Joe. *It's Anybody's Ballgame*. New York: Jove Books, 1988.

Garvey, Rev. Francis J. *Favorite Humor of Famous Americans*. Kandiyohi, Minnesota: Rev. Francis J. Garvey, 1981.

Gingras, Angele de T. *From Bussing to Bugging: The Best in Congressional Humor*. Washington, D.C.: Acropolis Books, Limited, 1973.

Gorman, Tom, and Jerome Holtzman. *Three and Two!* New York: Charles Scribner's Sons, 1979.

Green, Amy Boothe, and Howard E. Green. *Remembering Walt: Favorite Memories of Walt Disney*. New York: Disney Editions, 1999.

Greenberg, Keith Elliot. *Pro Wrestling: From Carnivals to Cable TV*. Minneapolis, MN: Lerner Publications Company, 2000.

Gregg, Eric, and Marty Appel. *Working the Plate: The Eric Gregg Story*. New York: William Morrow and Company, Inc., 1990.

Haney, Lynn. *The Lady is a Jock*. New York: Dodd, Mead, and Company, 1973.

Haney, Lynn. *Skaters: Profile of a Pair*. New York: G.P. Putnam's Sons, 1983.

Hanna, Edward; Henry Hicks; and Ted Koppel, compilers. *The Wit and Wisdom of Adlai Stevenson*. New York: Hawthorn Books, Inc., 1965.

Harris, Leon A. *The Fine Art of Political Wit*. New York: Dell Publishing Company, 1964.

Himelstein, Shmuel. *A Touch of Wisdom, A Touch of Wit*. Brooklyn, NY: Mesorah Publications, Limited, 1991.

Himelstein, Shmuel. *Words of Wisdom, Words of Wit*. Brooklyn, NY: Mesorah Publications, Ltd., 1993.

Horowitz, Susan. *Queens of Comedy*. Australia: Gordon and Breach Publishers, 1997.

Hyman, Dick. *Potomac Wind and Wisdom: Jokes, Lies, and True Stories By and About America's Politics and Politicians*. Brattleboro, Vermont: The Stephen Greene Press, 1980.

Johnson, Harry "Steamboat." *Standing the Gaff: The Life and Hard Times of a Minor League Umpire*. Introduction to the Bison Book edition by Larry R. Gerlach. Lincoln, NE: University of Nebraska Press, 1994.

Kettlewell, Ken. *Presidential Passages*. Lima, Ohio: Fairway Press, 2004.

Klinger, Kurt, collector. *A Pope Laughs: Stories of John XXIII*. Translated by Sally McDevitt Cunneen. New York: Holt, Rinehart and Winston, 1964.

Kolasky, John, collector and compiler. *Look, Comrade — The People are Laughing* .... Toronto, Ontario: Peter Martin Associates, Limited, 1972.

Lazar, David, editor. *Conversations with M.F.K. Fisher*. Jackson, Mississippi: University of Mississippi Press, 1992.

Lessa, Christina. *Gymnastics Balancing Acts*. New York: Universe Publishing, 1997.

Lessa, Christina. *Women Who Win: Stories of Triumph in Sport and in Life*. New York: Universe Publishing, 1998.

Mackenzie, Richard. *A Wee Nip at the 19th Hole: A History of the St. Andrews Caddie*. Chelsea, MI: Sleeping Bear Press, 1997.

Maltin, Leonard. *Movie Comedy Teams*. New York: The New American Library, Inc., 1970.

Mandelbaum, Yitta Halberstam. *Holy Brother: Inspiring Stories and Enchanted Tales About Rabbi Shlomo Carlebach*. Northvale, NJ: Jason Aronson, Inc., 1997.

Marx, Arthur. *Life With Groucho*. New York: Simon and Schuster, 1954.

Marx, Arthur. *Son of Groucho*. New York: David McKay Company, Inc., 1972.

Mendelsohn, S. Felix. *Here's a Good One: Stories of Jewish Wit and Wisdom*. New York: Block Publishing Co., 1947.

Michaels, Louis. *The Humor and Warmth of Pope John XXIII: His Anecdotes and Legends*. New York: Pocket Books, Inc., 1965.

Miller, Ernestine Gichner. *The Babe Book*. Kansas City, MO: Andrews McMeel Publishing, 2000.

Milligan, Spike. *Adolf Hitler: My Part in His Downfall*. London: Michael Joseph, Limited, 1971.

Molen, Sam. *Take 2 and Hit to Right*. Philadelphia, PA: Dorrance and Company, 1959.

Morgan, David. *Monty Python Speaks*. New York: Avon Books, Inc., 1999.

Morgan, Henry. *Here's Morgan!* New York: Barricade Books, Inc., 1994.

Morton, Robert, editor. *Stand-up Comedians on Television*. New York: Harry N. Abrams, Inc. [in association with] The Museum of Television & Radio, 1996.

Mostel, Kate, and Madeline Gilford. *170 Years of Show Business*. With Jack Gilford and Zero Mostel. New York: Random House, 1978.

Mostel, Zero, and Max Waldman. *Zero by Mostel*. New York: Horizon Press, 1965.

Muallimoglu, Nejat. *The Wit and Wisdom of Nasraddin Hodja*. New York: Cynthia Parzych Publishing, Inc., 1986.

Mullen, Tom. *Laughing Out Loud and Other Religious Experiences*. Waco, TX: Word Books, 1983.

Nachman, Gerald. *Seriously Funny: The Rebel Comedians of the 1950s and 1960s*. New York: Pantheon Books, 2003.

Oakie, Victoria Horne, compiler and editor. *"Dear Jack": Hollywood Birthday Reminiscences to Jack Oakie*. Portland, Oregon: Strawberry Hill Press, 1994.

Orleans, Ellen. *Who Cares If It's a Choice?* Bala Cynwyd, PA: Laugh Lines Press, 1994.

Parker, John F. *"If Elected, I Promise ...."* Garden City, NY: Doubleday & Co., Inc., 1960.

Pellowski, Michael J. *Baseball's Funniest People*. New York: Sterling Publishing Co., 1997.

Peterson, T.F. *Nightwork: A History of Hacks and Pranks at MIT*. Cambridge, Massachusetts: MIT Press, 2011.

Poley, Irvin C., and Ruth Verlenden Poley. *Friendly Anecdotes*. New York: Harper & Brothers, Publishers, 1950.

Porter, Alyene. *Papa was a Preacher*. New York: Abingdon Press, 1944.

Primack, Ben, adapter and editor. *The Ben Hecht Show: Impolitic Observations from the Freest Thinker of 1950s Television*. Jefferson, NC: McFarland & Company, Inc., Publishers, 1993.

Rayner, William P. *Wise Women*. New York: St. Martin's Press, 1983.

Reef, Catherine. *Paul Laurence Dunbar: Portrait of a Poet*. Berkeley Heights, NJ: Enslow Publications, Inc., 2000.

Retton, Mary Lou, and Bela Karolyi. *Mary Lou: Creating an Olympic Champion*. With John Powers. New York: McGraw-Hill Book Company, 1986.

Richards, Dick, compiler. *The Wit of Noël Coward*. London: Leslie Frewin, 1968.

Rodriguez-Hunter, Suzanne. *Found Meals of the Lost Generation*. Boston, MA: Faber and Faber, 1994.

Rogers, Fred. *The World According to Mister Rogers*. New York: Hyperion, 2003.

Rowell, Edward K., editor. *Humor for Preaching and Teaching*. Grand Rapids, MI: Baker Books, 1996.

Ruksenas, Algis. *Is That You Laughing Comrade? The World's Best Russian (Underground) Jokes*. Secaucus, NJ: Citadel Press, 1986.

Russell, Fred. *I'll Try Anything Twice*. Nashville, TN: The McQuiddy Press, 1945.

Russell, Mark, editor. *Out of Character*. New York: Bantam Books, 1997.

Rutkowska, Wanda. *Famous People in Anecdotes*. Warszawa: Wydawnictwa Szkolne i Pedagogiczne, 1977.

Rutledge, Rachel. *The Best of the Best in Gymnastics*. Brookfield, CT: The Millbrook Press, 1999.

Salzberg, Sharon. *A Heart as Wide as the World: Stories on the Path to Lovingkindness*. Boston, MA: Shambhala Publications, Inc., 1997.

Samra, Cal and Rose, editors. *Holy Hilarity*. Colorado Springs, CO: WaterBrook Press, 1999.

Samra, Cal and Rose, editors. *More Holy Hilarity*. Colorado Springs, CO: WaterBrook Press, 1999.

Savage, Jeff. *Julie Foudy: Soccer Superstar*. Minneapolis, MN: Lerner Publications Company, 1999.

Savage, Jeff. *Tiger Woods: King of the Course*. Minneapolis, MN: Lerner Publications Company, 1998.

Sessions, William H., collector. *Laughter in Quaker Grey*. York, England: William Sessions, Limited, 1966.

Sessions, William H., collector. *More Quaker Laughter*. York, England: William Sessions, Limited, 1974.

Shah, Idries. *The Subtleties of the Inimitable Mulla Nasrudin*. London: The Octagon Press, 1983.

Silverman, Stephen M. *Funny Ladies: The Women Who Make Us Laugh*. New York: Harry N. Abrams, Inc., 1999.

Silverman, William B. *Rabbinic Wisdom and Jewish Values*. New York: Union of American Hebrew Congregations, 1971.

Skipper, John C. *Umpires: Classic Baseball Stories from the Men Who Made the Calls*. Jefferson, NC, and London: McFarland and Company, Inc., Publishers, 1997.

Slide, Anthony. *Eccentrics of Comedy*. Lanham, MD, and London: The Scarecrow Press, Inc., 1998.

Smith, Beverley. *Figure Skating: A Celebration*. Toronto, Ontario, Canada: McClelland & Stewart, Inc., 1994.

Smith, Bob. *Openly Bob*. New York: William Morrow and Company, Inc., 1997.

Smith, Bob. *Way to Go, Smith!* New York: HarperCollins Publishers, Inc., 1999.

Szilard, Paul. *Under My Wings: My Life as an Impresario*. New York: Limelight Editions, 2002.

Smith, Ira L. and H. Allen Smith. *Low and Inside*. Garden City, NY: Doubleday and Company, Inc., 1949.

Smith, Ira L., and H. Allen Smith. *Three Men on Third*. New York: Doubleday & Co., Inc., 1951.

Smith, Ron. *Comic Support*. New York: Carol Publishing Group, 1993.

Snead, Sam. *The Game I Love: Wisdom, Insight, and Instruction from Golf's Greatest Player*. With Fran Pirozzolo. New York: Ballantine Books, 1997.

Sobol, Donald J. *Encyclopedia Brown's Book of Wacky Sports*. New York: William Morrow and Company, 1984.

Stephens, Autumn. *Feisty First Ladies and Other Unforgettable White House Women*. San Francisco, California: Viva Editions, 2009.

Stephens, Autumn. *Wild Women in the White House*. Berkeley, CA: Conari Press, 1997.

Stone, Laurie. *Laughing in the Dark: A Decade of Subversive Comedy*. Hopewell, New Jersey: The Ecco Press, 1997.

Taylor, Robert Lewis. *W.C. Fields: His Follies and Fortunes*. Garden City, NY: Doubleday and Company, Inc., 1949.

Terry-Thomas, and Terry Daum. *Terry-Thomas ... Tells Tales*. London: Robson Books, 1990.

Thomas, Bob. *Bud & Lou: The Abbott and Costello Story*. Philadelphia, PA: J.B. Lippincott Company, 1977.

Took, Barry. *Comedy Greats: A Celebration of Comic Genius Past and Present*. Wellingborough, Northamptonshire, England: Equation, 1989.

Towse, John Rankin. *Sixty Years of the Theater: An Old Critic's Memories*. New York and London: Funk & Wagnalls Company, 1916.

Troy, Con. *Laugh with Hugh Troy, World's Greatest Practical Joker*. Wyomissing, PA: Trojan Books, 1983.

Udall, Morris K. *Too Funny to be President*. With Bob Neuman and Randy Udall. New York: Henry Holt and Company, 1988.

Uecker, Bob, and Mickey Herskowitz. *Catcher in the Wry*. New York: G.P. Putnam's Sons, 1982.

Unterbrink, Mary. *Funny Women: American Comediennes, 1860-1985*. Jefferson, NC: McFarland and Co., Inc., Publishers, 1987.

Wade, Don. *"And Then Arnie Told Chi Chi ...."* Chicago, IL: Contemporary Books, 1993.

Warren, Roz, editor. *Revolutionary Laughter: The World of Women Comics*. Freedom, CA: The Crossing Press, 1995.

Weatherby, W.J. *Jackie Gleason: An Intimate Portrait*. New York: Berkley Books, 1992.

Wiesel, Elie. *Souls on Fire: Portraits and Legends of Hasidic Masters*. Translated from the French by Marion Wiesel. New York: Random House, 1972.

Wilde, Larry. *The Great Comedians*. Secaucus, NJ: The Citadel Press, 1968.

Williams, John A., and Dennis A. Williams. *If I Stop I'll Die: The Comedy and Tragedy of Richard Pryor*. New York: Thunder's Mouth Press, 1991.

Wordsworth, R. D., compiler. *"Abe" Lincoln's Anecdotes and Stories*. Boston, MA: The Mutual Book Company, 1908.

Zall, P. M. *George Washington Laughing: Humorous Anecdotes by and about our first President from Original Sources*. Hamden, CN: Archon Books, 1989.

Zall, Paul M. *The Wit and Wisdom of the Founding Fathers*. Hopewell, New Jersey: The Ecco Press, 1996.

Zimmerman, Paul D., and Burt Goldblatt. *The Marx Brothers at the Movies*. New York: G.P. Putnam's Sons, 1968.

Appendix B: About the Author

It was a dark and stormy night. Suddenly a cry rang out, and on a hot summer night in 1954, Josephine, wife of Carl Bruce, gave birth to a boy — me. Unfortunately, this young married couple allowed Reuben Saturday, Josephine's brother, to name their first-born. Reuben, aka "The Joker," decided that Bruce was a nice name, so he decided to name me Bruce Bruce. I have gone by my middle name — David — ever since.

Being named Bruce David Bruce hasn't been all bad. Bank tellers remember me very quickly, so I don't often have to show an ID. It can be fun in charades, also. When I was a counselor as a teenager at Camp Echoing Hills in Warsaw, Ohio, a fellow counselor gave the signs for "sounds like" and "two words," then she pointed to a bruise on her leg twice. Bruise Bruise? Oh yeah, Bruce Bruce is the answer!

Uncle Reuben, by the way, gave me a haircut when I was in kindergarten. He cut my hair short and shaved a small bald spot on the back of my head. My mother wouldn't let me go to school until the bald spot grew out again.

Of all my brothers and sisters (six in all), I am the only transplant to Athens, Ohio. I was born in Newark, Ohio, and have lived all around Southeastern Ohio. However, I moved to Athens to go to Ohio University and have never left.

At Ohio U, I never could make up my mind whether to major in English or Philosophy, so I got a bachelor's degree with a double major in both areas, then I added a Master of Arts degree in English and a Master of Arts degree in Philosophy. Yes, I have my MAMA degree.

At Ohio U, I never could make up my mind whether to major in English or Philosophy, so I got a bachelor's degree with a double major in both areas, then I added a Master of Arts degree in English and a Master of Arts degree in Philosophy. Yes, I have my MAMA degree.

Currently, and for a long time to come (I eat fruits and veggies), I am spending my retirement writing books such as *Nadia Comaneci: Perfect 10*, *The Funniest People in Comedy*, *Homer's* Iliad: *A Retelling in Prose*, and *William Shakespeare's* Hamlet: *A Retelling in Prose*.

By the way, my sister Brenda Kennedy writes romances such as *A New Beginning* and *Shattered Dreams*.

Appendix C: Some Books by David Bruce

Anecdote Collections

250 Anecdotes About Opera
250 Anecdotes About Religion
250 Anecdotes About Religion: Volume 2
250 Music Anecdotes
Be a Work of Art: 250 Anecdotes and Stories
The Coolest People in Art: 250 Anecdotes
The Coolest People in the Arts: 250 Anecdotes
The Coolest People in Books: 250 Anecdotes
The Coolest People in Comedy: 250 Anecdotes
Create, Then Take a Break: 250 Anecdotes
Don't Fear the Reaper: 250 Anecdotes
The Funniest People in Art: 250 Anecdotes
The Funniest People in Books: 250 Anecdotes
The Funniest People in Books, Volume 2: 250 Anecdotes
The Funniest People in Books, Volume 3: 250 Anecdotes
The Funniest People in Comedy: 250 Anecdotes
The Funniest People in Dance: 250 Anecdotes
The Funniest People in Families: 250 Anecdotes
The Funniest People in Families, Volume 2: 250 Anecdotes
The Funniest People in Families, Volume 3: 250 Anecdotes
The Funniest People in Families, Volume 4: 250 Anecdotes
The Funniest People in Families, Volume 5: 250 Anecdotes
The Funniest People in Families, Volume 6: 250 Anecdotes
The Funniest People in Movies: 250 Anecdotes
The Funniest People in Music: 250 Anecdotes
The Funniest People in Music, Volume 2: 250 Anecdotes
The Funniest People in Music, Volume 3: 250 Anecdotes
The Funniest People in Neighborhoods: 250 Anecdotes
The Funniest People in Relationships: 250 Anecdotes
The Funniest People in Sports: 250 Anecdotes
The Funniest People in Sports, Volume 2: 250 Anecdotes
The Funniest People in Television and Radio: 250 Anecdotes
The Funniest People in Theater: 250 Anecdotes

The Funniest People Who Live Life: 250 Anecdotes
The Funniest People Who Live Life, Volume 2: 250 Anecdotes
The Kindest People Who Do Good Deeds, Volume 1: 250 Anecdotes
The Kindest People Who Do Good Deeds, Volume 2: 250 Anecdotes
Maximum Cool: 250 Anecdotes
The Most Interesting People in Movies: 250 Anecdotes
The Most Interesting People in Politics and History: 250 Anecdotes
The Most Interesting People in Politics and History, Volume 2: 250 Anecdotes
The Most Interesting People in Politics and History, Volume 3: 250 Anecdotes
The Most Interesting People in Religion: 250 Anecdotes
The Most Interesting People in Sports: 250 Anecdotes
The Most Interesting People Who Live Life: 250 Anecdotes
The Most Interesting People Who Live Life, Volume 2: 250 Anecdotes
Reality is Fabulous: 250 Anecdotes and Stories
Resist Psychic Death: 250 Anecdotes
Seize the Day: 250 Anecdotes and Stories

[1] Source: "Barbie Liberation Organisation." YouTube. 15 September 2010 <http://www.youtube.com/ watch?feature=player_embedded&v=eMHMf9y-27w>.

[2] Source: Ana Samways, "April 27: The hot tub." Sideswipe. *New Zealand Herald.* 27 April 2012 <http://www.nzherald.co.nz/sideswipe-with-ana-samways/news/article.cfm?c_id=1503050&objectid=10801660>.

[3] Source: Don Wade, *"And Then Arnie Told Chi Chi...,"* p. 68.

[4] Source: Roger Ebert, "Michael Caine's Just Eating It Up." *Chicago Sun-Times.* 6 December 1998. <http://rogerebert.suntimes.com/apps/pbcs.dll/ article?AID=/19981206/PEOPLE/212010326>.

[5] Source: Gyles Brandreth, *Great Theatrical Disasters*, pp. 64-65.

[6] Source: John Rankin Towse, *Sixty Years of the Theater: An Old Critic's Memories*, p. 79.

[7] Source: Jim and Henny Backus, *Forgive Us Our Digressions*, p. 145.

[8] Source: Victoria Horne Oakie, compiler and editor, *"Dear Jack,"* pp. 34, 130.

[9] Source: David Morgan, *Monty Python Speaks*, p. 87-90.

[10] Source: Henry Morgan, *Here's Morgan!*, pp. 177-179.

[11] Source: Joy Wallace Dickinson, *Remembering Orlando: Tales from Elvis to Disney*, pp. 67-69.

[12] Source: Robert Lewis Taylor, *W.C. Fields: His Follies and Fortunes*, pp. 163-164.

[13] Source: William H. Sessions, collector, *Laughter in Quaker Grey*, p. 56.

[14] Source: Suzanne Rodriguez-Hunter, *Found Meals of the Lost Generation*, p. 188.

[15] Source: Autumn Stephens, *Wild Women in the White House*, p. 75.

[16] Source: Amy Boothe Green and Howard E. Green, *Remembering Walt: Favorite Memories of Walt Disney*, pp. 49, 174.

[17] Source: Idries Shah, *The Subtleties of the Inimitable Mulla Nasrudin*, p. 84.

[18] Source: Michael J. Pellowski, *Baseball's Funniest People*, pp. 8-9.

[19] Source: Ana Samways, "June 18: Radio lookalikes." Sideswipe. *New Zealand Herald.* 18 June 2012 <http://www.nzherald.co.nz/ana-samways/news/article.cfm?a_id=53&objectid=10813659>.

[20] Source: Christina Martin, "A dog texts the Metro Good Deed Feed." *Anorak* (UK). 29 June 2012 <http://www.anorak.co.uk/326539/news/a-dog-texts-the-metro-good-deed-feed.html/>.

[21] Source: Davis Lazar, editor, *Conversations with M.F.K. Fisher*, pp. 56, 61, 80, 107.

[22] Source: John C. Skipper, *Umpires*, p. 133.

[23] Source: Shmuel Himelstein, *A Touch of Wisdom, A Touch of Wit*, p. 29.

[24] Source: Taylor Plimpton, "My Father's Voice." *New Yorker.* 17 June 2012 <http://www.newyorker.com/online/blogs/books/2012/06/george-plimptons-voice.html>.

[25] Source: Jocko Conlan and Robert W. Creamer, *Jocko*, p. 190.

[26] Source: Joe Garagiola, *It's Anybody's Ballgame*, pp. 103-104.

[27] Source: Joe Garagiola, *Baseball is a Funny Game*, pp. 69-70, 86.

[28] Source: Bob Uecker and Mickey Herskowitz, *Catcher in the Wry*, pp. 195, 197.

[29] Source: Sam Molen, *Take 2 and Hit to Right*, pp. 14, 20-21.

[30] Source: "Young Baseball Fan's Act of Generosity." ABCNews YouTube. 22 July 2011 <http://www.youtube.com/watch?v=QfF1m3-Dl_Q>.

[31] Source: Harry "Steamboat" Johnson, *Standing the Gaff*, pp. 65-66.

[32] Source: Joe Garagiola, *Baseball is a Funny Game*, p. 41.

[33] Source: Ira L. Smith and H. Allen Smith, *Three Men on Third*, pp. 134-135.

[34] Source: Sam Molen, *Take 2 and Hit to Right*, pp. 55, 160.

[35] Source: Michael J. Pellowski, *Baseball's Funniest People*, p. 49.

[36] Source: Yogi Berra, *"I Really Didn't Say Everything I Said,"* pp. 56, 73.

[37] Source: Eric Gregg and Marty Appel, *Working the Plate*, p. 149.

[38] Source: "Mom gives birth on train headed to hospital." CNN. Todaysthv.com. 18 January 2012 **<http://www.todaysthv.com/news/story.aspx?storyid=191106>**.

[39] Source: Davis Lazar, editor, *Conversations with M.F.K. Fisher*, pp. 180, 197.

[40] Source: Autumn Stephens, *Feisty First Ladies and Other Unforgettable White House Women*, p. 130.

[41] Source: Jeff Savage, *Julie Foudy: Soccer Superstar*, pp. 19, 21.

[42] Source: Ken Alley, *Awkward Christian Soldiers*, pp. 38-39.

[43] Source: William H. Sessions, collector, *More Quaker Laughter*, pp. 22-23.

[44] Source: Barry Took, *Comedy Greats*, p. 219.

[45] Source: Edward K. Rowell, editor, *Humor for Preaching and Teaching*, p. 168.

[46] Source: Alyene Porter, *Papa was a Preacher*, p. 167.

[47] Source: Bill Crow, *Jazz Anecdotes*, p. 25.

[48] Source: Edward Hanna, Henry Hicks, and Ted Koppel, compilers, *The Wit and Wisdom of Adlai Stevenson*, p. 81.

[49] Source: "Dress, 1-Piece: Catalogue number: 1992.0236.001; Date: 1947." Smithsonian. **<http://americanhistory.si.edu/collections/costume/object.cfm?recordnumber=834994>**.

[50] Source: Kurt Klinger, *A Pope Laughs*, pp. 22-24.

[51] Source: William H. Sessions, collector, *More Quaker Laughter*, pp. 6, 9.

[52] Source: P. M. Zall, *George Washington Laughing*, p. 37.

[53] Source: Bob Thomas, *Bud & Lou*, pp. 88, 103, 163.

[54] Source: Ron Smith, *Comic Support*, pp. 8-9, 125, 137, 219.

[55] Source: Barry Took, *Comedy Greats*, pp. 158-159.

[56] Source: Bob Smith, *Openly Bob*, p. 95. Also: Bob Smith, *Way to Go, Smith!*, pp. 26, 216-217.

[57] Source: Terry-Thomas, *Terry-Thomas Tells Tales*, pp. 12, 42.

[58] Source: Gerald Nachman, *Seriously Funny*, pp. 161, 163.

[59] Source: Anthony Slide, *Eccentrics of Comedy*, pp. 138-139, 142.

[60] Source: Arthur Marx, *Life With Groucho*, pp. 92-94.

[61]Source: Paul D. Zimmerman and Burt Goldblatt, *The Marx Brothers at the Movies*, p. 14.

[62]Source: Susan Horowitz, *Queens of Comedy*, p. 155.

[63]Source: Larry Wilde, *The Great Comedians*, pp. 70-71, 212.

[64]Source: Arthur Marx, *Son of Groucho*, p. 354.

[65]Source: Victoria Horne Oakie, compiler and editor, *"Dear Jack,"* Editor's Note and p. 31.

[66]Source: Henry Morgan, *Here's Morgan!*, p. 135.

[67]Source: Mary Unterbrink, *Funny Women*, pp. 211-213.

[68]Source: Gerald Nachman, *Seriously Funny*, pp. 66, 79.

[69]Source: Leonard Maltin, *Movie Comedy Teams*, p. 342.

[70]Source: Anthony Slide, *Eccentrics of Comedy*, p. 6.

[71]Source: Robert Morton, editor, *Stand-up Comedians on Television*, p. 102.

[72]Source: Tom Mullen, *Laughing Out Loud and Other Religious Experiences*, p. 44.

[73] Source: Benjamin R. Freed, "Craigslist Vendor Caught Dealing Stolen Bikes." *DCist.* 8 May 2012 **<http://dcist.com/2012/05/craigslist_vendor_caught_dealing_st.php>**.

[74]Source: Yitta Halberstam Mandelbaum, *Holy Brother*, p. 147-148.

[75]Source: Keith Elliot Greenberg, *Pro Wrestling: From Carnivals to Cable TV*, p. 100.

[76]Source: Ben Primack, adapter and editor, *The Ben Hecht Show*, p. 187, 197.

[77]Source: Wanda Rutkowska, *Famous People in Anecdotes*, p. 11.

[78]Source: James Fadiman and Robert Frager, *Essential Sufism*, p. 255.

[79]Source: Ben Primack, adapter and editor, *The Ben Hecht Show*, p. 184.

[80] Source: Adam K. Raymond, "Imaginary Friends: 5 Really Successful People Who Never Really Existed[1]." Mental Floss. 13 May 2011 **<http://www.mentalfloss.com/blogs/archives/87027>**. Also: "George P. Burdell." Georgia Tech Alumni. **<http://gtalumni.org/Publications/magazine/spr98/div02.html>**. Accessed 1 May 2012. Also: "George P. Burdell." Wikipedia. **<http://en.wikipedia.org/wiki/George_P._Burdell>**. Accessed 1 May 2012.

---

1.   http://www.mentalfloss.com/blogs/archives/87027

Source: Web Credits. South Park Studios. **<http://www.southparkstudios.com/about/web-credits>**. Accessed 1 May 2012.

[81] Source: Rose Eichenbaum, *Masters of Movement: Portraits of America's Great Choreographers*, pp. 42-43.

[82]Source: Sharon Salzberg, *A Heart as Wide as the World*, pp. 140-141, 156, 191-192.

[83] Source: Rose Eichenbaum, *Masters of Movement: Portraits of America's Great Choreographers*, pp. 5-6.

[84] Source: Louis Peitzman, "Fifth Grader Gets Presidential Pardon for Absence." Gawker. 2 June 2012 **<http://gawker.com/5915149/fifth-grader-gets-presidential-pardon-for-absence>**.

[85]Source: Angele de T. Gingras, *From Bussing to Bugging*, p. 28.

[86]Source: Sharon Salzberg, *Lovingkindness*, p. 154.

[87]Source: John A. Williams and Dennis A. Williams, *If I Stop I'll Die*, pp. 25, 218.

[88] Source: "Nguyen for the Win!" Neatorama. 17 May 2012 **<http://www.neatorama.com/2012/05/17/nguyen-for-the-win/>**.

[89]Source: Sharon Salzberg, *Lovingkindness*, p. 87.

[90]Source: Kurt Klinger, *A Pope Laughs*, p. 56.

[91]Source: Idries Shah, *The Subtleties of the Inimitable Mulla Nasrudin*, p. 4.

[92]Source: Nejat Muallimoglu, *The Wit and Wisdom of Nasraddin Hodja*, p. 53.

[93]Source: Ernestine Gichner Miller, *The Babe Book*, p. 91.

[94]Source: Nate Aaseng, *Great Winter Olympic Moments*, pp. 13, 59, 63.

[95]Source: W.J. Weatherby, *Jackie Gleason: An Intimate Portrait*, pp. 10, 66-67.

[96] Source: "The Graveyard Of Shelved Ice Cream Flavors." NPR. 28 May 2012 **<http://www.npr.org/2012/05/28/153602928/the-graveyard-of-shelved-ice-cream-flavors>**.

[97] Source: Amy Boothe Green and Howard E. Green, *Remembering Walt: Favorite Memories of Walt Disney*, pp. 25, 36, 38.

[98]Source: Bob Uecker and Mickey Herskowitz, *Catcher in the Wry*, p. 166.

[99]Source: Elie Wiesel, *Souls on Fire*, p. 99.

[100]Source: Leila Merrell Foster, *Benjamin Franklin: Founding Father and Inventor*, p. 41.

[101]Source: Paul M. Zall, *The Wit and Wisdom of the Founding Fathers*, p. 44.

[102]Source: Autumn Stephens, *Wild Women in the White House*, p. 96.

[103] Source: T.F. Peterson, *Nightwork: A History of Hacks and Pranks at MIT*, p. 124.

[104]Source: Massud Farzan, *Another Way of Laughter*, p. 46.

[105]Source: David Morgan, *Monty Python Speaks*, p. 28.

[106]Source: Kate Mostel and Madeline Gilford, *170 Years of Show Business*, p. 8.

[107]Source: Bob Dole, *Great Political Wit*, p. 176.

[108]Source: Tom Mullen, *Laughing Out Loud and Other Religious Experiences*, p. 101.

[109]Source: Bob Smith, *Openly Bob*, p. 29. Also: Bob Smith, *Way to Go, Smith!*, pp. 5, 40, 169.

[110]Source: Ellen Orleans, *Who Cares If It's a Choice?*, pp. 20, 75.

[111]Source: Mark Russell, editor, *Out of Character*, pp. 198, 260.

[112]Source: Roz Warren, editor, *Revolutionary Laughter*, p. 110.

[113] Source: Ken Kettlewell, *Presidential Passages*, pp. 5, 51, 65.

[114]Source: Tom Gorman and Jerome Holtzman, *Three and Two!*, p. 71.

[115]Source: Fred Rogers, *The World According to Mister Rogers*, p. 118.

[116]Source: Jeff Savage, *Tiger Woods: King of the Course*, pp. 10, 15, 18-19, 52.

[117]Source: Don Wade, *"And Then Arnie Told Chi Chi...,"* p. 124.

[118]Source: Fred Russell, *I'll Try Anything Twice*, pp. 57, 59.

[119]Source: Donald J. Sobol, *Encyclopedia Brown's Book of Wacky Sports*, p. 104.

[120]Source: Sam Snead, *The Game I Love*, pp. 186-187.

[121] Source: Perry Backus, "Clinton girl donates birthday presents to horse rescue shelter." *Missoulian* (Missoula, Montana). 14 May 2012 <http://missoulian.com/news/local/clinton-girl-donates-birthday-presents-to-horse-rescue-shelter/article_4e6b38a4-9d75-11e1-aee3-001a4bcf887a.html>.

[122] Source: Anthony Bond, "'I'm just an average person': 20-year-old becomes the youngest ever Good Samaritan organ donor in Britain after giving his kidney to a complete stranger." *Daily Mail* (UK). 29 July 2012; updated 30 July 2012 <http://www.dailymail.co.uk/news/article-2180683/Sam-Nagy-20-gives-stranger-kidney-youngest-Good-Samaritan-organ-donor-Britain.html?ITO=1490>.

[123] Source: Simon Tomlinson, "The parking meter angel: Meet the Good Samaritan who will buy you a ticket when the traffic wardens are hovering." *Daily Mail* (UK). 20 June 2012 <http://www.dailymail.co.uk/news/article-2161939/The-parking-meter-angel-Meet-Good-Samaritan-buy-ticket-traffic-wardens-hovering.html>.

[124]Source: Nejat Muallimoglu, *The Wit and Wisdom of Nasraddin Hodja*, pp. 102-104.

[125]Source: William H. Sessions, collector, *Laughter in Quaker Grey*, p. 26.

[126] Source: Autumn Stephens, *Feisty First Ladies and Other Unforgettable White House Women*, pp. 168-169.

[127]Source: Edward K. Rowell, editor, *Humor for Preaching and Teaching*, p. 112.

[128]Source: Cal and Rose Samra, *More Holy Hilarity*, p. 39.

[129]Source: Suzanne Rodriguez-Hunter, *Found Meals of the Lost Generation*, pp. 68, 70-71.

[130]Source: Yogi Berra, *"I Really Didn't Say Everything I Said,"* book jacket, p. 22.

[131]Source: Laurie Stone, *Laughing in the Dark*, pp. 95, 108-109.

[132]Source: Ron Smith, *Comic Support*, p. 128.

[133]Source: Roz Warren, editor, *Revolutionary Laughter*, p. 248.

[134]Source: Morris K. Udall, *Too Funny to be President*, p. 226.

[135]Source: Fred Russell, *I'll Try Anything Twice*, p. 15

[136]Source: Gyles Brandreth, *Great Theatrical Disasters*, p. 101.

[137]Source: William P. Rayner, *Wise Women*, p. 185.

[138] Source: Tanaquil Le Clercq, *The Ballet Cook Book*, p. 223.

[139]Source: Arthur Marx, *Son of Groucho*, pp. 94, 354.

[140]Source: Keith Elliot Greenberg, *Pro Wrestling: From Carnivals to Cable TV*, pp. 39-40.

[141]Source: W.J. Weatherby, *Jackie Gleason: An Intimate Portrait*, pp. 113, 198.

[142]Source: Richard Mackenzie, *A Wee Nip at the 19th Hole*, p. 91.

[143]Source: Jeff Savage, *Julie Foudy: Soccer Superstar*, pp. 33-34.

[144]Source: Paul Szilard, *Under My Wings*, pp. 134-135.

[145]Source: Sam Snead, *The Game I Love*, p. 157.

[146] Source: Zero Mostel and Max Waldman, *Zero by Mostel*, unnumbered page in "Some Personal Words and Drawings."

[147]Source: Paul D. Zimmerman and Burt Goldblatt, *The Marx Brothers at the Movies*, p. 99.

[148]Source: Cal and Rose Samra, *Holy Hilarity*, p. 168.

[149]Source: Spike Milligan, *Adolf Hitler: My Part in His Downfall*, p. 128.

[150] Source: Jim and Henny Backus, *Forgive Us Our Digressions*, pp. 22-23.

[151]Source: Leonard Maltin, *Movie Comedy Teams*, p. 107.

[152] Source: Roger Ebert, Review of *Mission: Impossible — Ghost Protocol*. Suntimes.com. 14 December 2011 **<http://rogerebert.suntimes.com/apps/ pbcs.dll/article?AID=/20111214/REVIEWS/111219995>**.

[153]Source: John A. Williams and Dennis A. Williams, *If I Stop I'll Die*, pp. 208-209.

[154] Source: Bill Crow, *Jazz Anecdotes*, pp. 25-26.

[155]Source: John Deedy, *A Book of Catholic Anecdotes*, p. 248.

[156]Source: Mary Lou Retton and Bela Karolyi, *Mary Lou: Creating an Olympic Champion*, pp. 6, 60, 79.

[157]Source: Richard Mackenzie, *A Wee Nip at the 19th Hole*, pp. 90. 111.

[158]Source: Stephen M. Silverman, *Funny Ladies*, pp. 33, 75, 78.

[159]Source: Kate Mostel and Madeline Gilford, *170 Years of Show Business*, pp. 67-68, 90-91.

[160] Source: John Deedy, *A Book of Catholic Anecdotes*, p. 47.

[161]Source: Ernestine Gichner Miller, *The Babe Book*, p. 93.

[162]Source: Leon A. Harris, *The Fine Art of Political Wit*, pp. 142-143.

[163]Source: Bob Dole, *Great Presidential Wit*, p. 17.

[164]Source: John Kolasky, collector and compiler, *Look, Comrade — The People are Laughing…*, p. 92.

[165]Source: Paul M. Zall, *The Wit and Wisdom of the Founding Fathers*, p. 11.

[166]Source: Leila Merrell Foster, *Benjamin Franklin: Founding Father and Inventor*, p. 15.

[167]Source: Dick Hyman, *Potomac Wind and Wisdom*, p. 54.

[168]Source: Rev. Francis J. Garvey, *Favorite Humor of Famous Americans*, p. 4.

[169]Source: Angele de T. Gingras, *From Bussing to Bugging*, p. 110.

[170]Source: Harry "Steamboat" Johnson, *Standing the Gaff*, pp. 79-80.

[171] Source: T.F. Peterson, *Nightwork: A History of Hacks and Pranks at MIT*, p. 29.

[172] Source: "Save the Troy Library 'Adventures In Reverse Psychology." YouTube. Uploaded by LeoBurnettWorldwide on 15 November 2011 **<http://www.youtube.com/watch?v=nw3zNNO5gX0&feature=youtu.be>**. Also: Miss Cellania, "Burning Books to Save the Library." Neatorama. 15 June 2012 **<http://www.neatorama.com/2012/06/15/burning-books-to-save-the-library/>**. Also: "2012 Gold. GOODWORKS — NONPROFITS." Effie. Accessed 16 June 2012. [Link Broken] Troy Public Library. Book Burning Party. Effie. **https://www.effie.org/case_database/case/NA_2012_5940**

[173] Source: "Man who put resume on billboard gets a job." KARE (Minneapolis, Minnesota). 8 May 2012 **<http://www.kare11.com/news/article/975543/396/Man-who-put-resume-on-billboard-gets-a-job>**.

[174]Source: Joe Garagiola, *It's Anybody's Ballgame*, pp. 182-183.

[175]Source: Spike Milligan, *Adolf Hitler: My Part in His Downfall*, p. 68.

[176]Source: Lawrence J. Epstein, *A Treasury of Jewish Anecdotes*, p. 235.

[177] Source: Laura Barnett, "Frank Bowling and the politics of abstract painting." *Guardian* (UK). 2 July 2012 <http://www.guardian.co.uk/artanddesign/2012/jul/02/frank-bowling-abstract-artist-interview>.

[178]Source: Paul Szilard, *Under My Wings*, p. 80.

[179] Source: Tanaquil Le Clercq, *The Ballet Cook Book*, pp. 205-206.

[180]Source: Irvin C. Poley and Ruth Verlenden Poley, *Friendly Anecdotes*, p. 93.

[181]Source: S. Felix Mendelsohn, *Here's a Good One*, pp. 178-179.

[182]Source: Lawrence J. Epstein, *A Treasury of Jewish Anecdotes*, pp. 240-241.

[183]Source: Leon A. Harris, *The Fine Art of Political Wit*, p. 168.

[184]Source: Bob Dole, *Great Political Wit*, p. 12.

[185]Source: John F. Parker, *"If Elected, I Promise ...."*, p. 26.

[186]Source: Ken Alley, *Awkward Christian Soldiers*, p. 44, 47-48, 64, 67, 81, 92.

[187]Source: Beulah Collins, collector, *For Benefit of Clergy*, pp. 15, 30, 61, 66, 95.

[188]Source: Massud Farzan, *Another Way of Laughter*, pp. 4, 60.

[189]Source: Shmuel Himelstein, *A Touch of Wisdom, A Touch of Wit*, p. 187.

[190]Source: Shmuel Himelstein, *Words of Wisdom, Words of Wit*, p. 221.

[191]Source: Irvin C. Poley and Ruth Verlenden Poley, *Friendly Anecdotes*, pp. 116-117.

[192]Source: William B. Silverman, *Rabbinic Wisdom and Jewish Values*, pp. 206-207.

[193]Source: Joey Adams, *The God Bit*, p. 218.

[194]Source: Con Troy, *Laugh with Hugh Troy*, pp. 145-146.

[195]Source: Bob Thomas, *Bud & Lou*, pp. 28, 53.

[196]Source: Laurie Stone, *Laughing in the Dark*, p. 129.

[197]Source: Dick Hyman, *Potomac Wind and Wisdom*, pp. 48-49.

[198]Source: Arthur Marx, *Life With Groucho*, pp. 189-190.

[199]Source: Beverley Smith, *Figure Skating: A Celebration*, pp. 52-53, 72, 107, 150, 169.

[200]Source: Christine Brennan, *Inside Edge*, p. 172, 207, 272.

[201]Source: Christina Lessa, *Gymnastics Balancing Acts*, pp. 28, 52. 95.

[202]Source: Christina Lessa, *Women Who Win*, pp. 20, 26.

[203]Source: Beverley Smith, *Figure Skating: A Celebration*, pp. 74, 79.

[204]Source: Lynn Haney, *Skaters: Profile of a Pair*, pp. 30, 54.

[205]Source: Jeff Savage, *Tiger Woods: King of the Course*, pp. 47, 56.

[206]Source: Christina Lessa, *Women Who Win*, p. 73.

[207]Source: Rachel Rutledge, *The Best of the Best in Gymnastics*, pp. 41, 43.

[208]Source: Donald J. Sobol, *Encyclopedia Brown's Book of Wacky Sports*, p. 97.

[209]Source: Yitta Halberstam Mandelbaum, *Holy Brother*, p. 143-144.

[210]Source: Susan Horowitz, *Queens of Comedy*, pp. 66, 68, 128.

[211]Source: Terry-Thomas, *Terry-Thomas Tells Tales*, pp. 37-38.

[212]Source: Helen White Charles, collector and editor, *Quaker Chuckles*, pp. 64-65, 92-93.

[213]Source: Mary Unterbrink, *Funny Women*, pp. 52-53.

[214]Source: John C. Skipper, *Umpires*, pp. 8, 13-15.

[215]Source: Ira L. Smith and H. Allen Smith, *Low and Inside*, pp. 180-181.

[216]Source: Ira L. Smith and H. Allen Smith, *Three Men on Third*, pp. 18-19.

[217]Source: Jocko Conlan and Robert W. Creamer, *Jocko*, p. 66.

[218]Source: Tom Gorman and Jerome Holtzman, *Three and Two!*, pp. 72-73.

[219]Source: Eric Gregg and Marty Appel, *Working the Plate*, pp. 101-102.

[220]Source: Algis Ruksenas, *Is That You Laughing Comrade?*, pp. 115, 119.

[221]Source: John Kolasky, collector and compiler, *Look, Comrade — The People are Laughing ...*, p. 115.

[222]Source: Reggie Finlayson, *Colin Powell: People's Hero*, p. 21-22, 33-34.

[223]Source: R. D. Wordsworth, compiler, *"Abe" Lincoln's Anecdotes and Stories*, pp. 7, 23.

[224]Source: Con Troy, *Laugh with Hugh Troy*, p. 118.

[225]Source: Dick Richards, compiler, *The Wit of Noël Coward*, pp. 13, 37, 47, 65-66, 93.

[226]Source: James Fadiman and Robert Frager, *Essential Sufism*, pp. 75-76, 131.

[227]Source: Edward Hanna, Henry Hicks, and Ted Koppel, compilers, *The Wit and Wisdom of Adlai Stevenson*, pp. 36, 84, 86.

[228]Source: Steve Allen, *More Funny People*, pp. 30, 72.

[229]Source: Bob Dole, *Great Presidential Wit*, p. 14.

[230]Source: William B. Silverman, *Rabbinic Wisdom and Jewish Values*, pp. 5, 54.

[231]Source: Stephen M. Silverman, *Funny Ladies*, p. 30.

[232]Source: Helen White Charles, collector and editor, *Quaker Chuckles*, pp. 34-35.

[233]Source: John F. Parker, *"If Elected, I Promise ...."*, p. 147.

[234]Source: P. M. Zall, *George Washington Laughing*, p. 7.

[235]Source: Shmuel Himelstein, *Words of Wisdom, Words of Wit*, p. 157.

[236]Source: Morris K. Udall, *Too Funny to be President*, p. 99.

[237]Source: S. Felix Mendelsohn, *Here's a Good One*, pp. 222-223.

[238]Source: Elie Wiesel, *Souls on Fire*, p. 153.

[239] Source: Merrill Ashley, *Dancing for Balanchine*, pp. 122-123, 125, 148-149, 156-157.

[240]Source: Robert Lewis Taylor, *W.C. Fields: His Follies and Fortunes*, pp. 10, 30-31.

[241]Source: R. D. Wordsworth, compiler, *"Abe" Lincoln's Anecdotes and Stories*, p. 65.

[242]Source: Lynn Haney, *The Lady is a Jock*, photo section and p. 37.

[243]Source: Sandra Bezic, *The Passion to Skate*, pp. 109, 140, 144.

[244]Source: Catherine Reef, *Paul Laurence Dunbar: Portrait of a Poet*, pp. 8, 16-17, 75-76.

[245]Source: Lynn Haney, *The Lady is a Jock*, pp. 30, 58.

[246]Source: Robert Morton, editor, *Stand-up Comedians on Television*, pp. 66, 69.

[247]Source: Cal and Rose Samra, *More Holy Hilarity*, p. 165.

[248]Source: Louis Michaels, *The Humor and Warmth of Pope John XXIII*, pp. 7, 43-44.

[249]Source: Perle Besserman and Manfred Steger, *Crazy Clouds*, p. 14, 48, 170, 173, 183.

[250]Source: Sushila Blackman, compiler and editor, *Graceful Exits*, pp. 30-31, 76, 78.